Trouble Downtown
The Local Context of Twentieth-Century America

Trouble Downtown

The Local Context of Twentieth-Century America

Henry F. Bedford
Phillips Exeter Academy

Under the General Editorship of
John Morton Blum, Yale University

 HARCOURT BRACE JOVANOVICH, INC.
New York   San Diego   Chicago   San Francisco   Atlanta

For Kennie,
and it's long overdue

Frontispiece: Fernand Léger,
The City, 1919 (detail).
Philadelphia Museum of
Art (A. E. Gallatin Collection)

Maps by Jean Paul Tremblay

ISBN: 0-15-592369-2

Library of Congress Catalog Card Number: 77–85311

Printed in the United States of America

Preface

Trouble Downtown derives from my observation that undergraduate students of American history both enjoy and profit from an occasional shift of focus from national events to those on a smaller scale. The drama of identifiable individuals confronting specific difficulties in a troubled community engages students and enhances their comprehension and retention of historical concepts that may otherwise seem remote and abstract. For example, the ambivalent observations of one reporter, torn between his convictions about legal process and his sympathy for legally oppressed working people, may add much to a discussion of Progressivism.

Local history also helps students recognize the exceptions and qualifying phrases that historians sometimes leave unstated when they generalize about the nation's past. Texans, after all, differ from Pennsylvanians—a distinction that may be lost in observations about the political behavior of the American electorate. Like my classmates, I once learned that the presidential election of 1908 turned on the tariff. That generalization may accurately describe the motive of some voters, and perhaps students somewhere still learn it. But some years later, after reading newspapers published in 1908 in several small Massachusetts cities, I learned that statements about presidential elections require careful qualification. The voters I knew—those whose words appeared in the newspapers I was reading—had more interest in the hours of local saloons and the performance of the local sheriff than in import duties and William Howard Taft. They voted out of outrage or out of habit, whatever the candidate's stand on the tariff.

The local history in this book requires no major modification in the usual view of the nation's past. Indeed, I have chosen incidents to exemplify historical generalizations, not to contradict them. My selection may strike some readers as arbitrary, a judgment with which I have no serious quarrel. But each chapter, I believe, examines a topic that is important to an understanding of the nation's past, and each centers on interesting people and events. Those are the principles that guided my choices.

My collaborators on this project were legion, and not all of them are acknowledged either here or in the notes. I have not, for instance, listed the monographs and the journal articles that have shaped my view of each decade under discussion, nor have I ordinarily cluttered the notes with multiple citations to document a single point. Yet the notes do, I think, suggest sources for local history of this sort, as well as indicate a fraction of my dependence on other scholars.

Some of those scholars are colleagues and former colleagues at Phillips Exeter Academy. The Trustees and two principals, Richard W. Day and Stephen G. Kurtz, approved an indispensable sabbatical leave. Albert C. Ganley, Richard D. Schubart, and Francis L. Broderick (now of the University of Massachusetts, Boston) read and improved portions of the manuscript; Donald B. Cole edited all of it. My obligations to the staff of the Academy Library are large and varied: Donna Moore typed the entire draft when it would have been easier to tell me to go away; Mary Lee Worboys patiently taught me much about exploiting libraries and ingeniously turned up sources; Jacquelyn Thomas never visibly resented the fact that the librarians sometimes seemed to be working for me, even when I was supposed to be on leave. Hugh Pritchard, of the library at the University of New Hampshire, and Hamilton B. Webb, of the Library of Congress, also responded generously when I imposed on them.

John Morton Blum, of Yale University, the general editor of the Harbrace History of the United States, has guided this book from its inception; almost every page shows the result of his careful, detailed criticism. Michael Ebner, of Lake Forest College, also commented incisively on the whole manuscript. The advice of Sidney Fine, of the University of Michigan, helped with the chapter on

Detroit, and two long telephone calls from Joe Azbell clarified the chapter on Montgomery.

Perhaps there are publishers that serve their authors better than does Harcourt Brace Jovanovich, but I have never encountered one. Thomas A. Williamson and William J. Wisneski have nursed this book from idea to outline to manuscript. With tact and skill, Lee Shenkman has improved that manuscript. Working from the barest of clues, Carla Hirst Wiltenburg tracked down the illustrations. Laurel Miller and Helen McCarthy prepared and checked proof at its various stages. The errors that remain belong to me.

HENRY F. BEDFORD

Contents

INTRODUCTION
Of Parables and the Past

An experienced news editor or broadcaster instinctively sorts the day's stories into "local" and "national" categories. Yet in a longer view, that line between local and national blurs, for local events may have immediate national consequences, particularly in the twentieth century. Demonstrations, boycotts, strikes, and arrests may inspire imitators and sympathizers in other communities, and a local episode quickly matures as a national cause or movement.

The interaction of local events and national history is one theme of this book. Local incidents are at the center of each chapter, but they occur in a national context. In many of those chapters, events and circumstances are said to be typical of those elsewhere in the United States. The assertion that a place is "typical" serves as an impressionistic equivalent of the statistical tests more precise observers use to be sure a tiny sample represents some larger population. Neither test is infallible, but one may produce a mathematical model of some aspect of life, and the other an illuminating metaphor.

The chapters that follow are intended as metaphors. Each describes events in one community, but those events absorbed the nation's attention because, with local variations, they might have happened anywhere. A great textile strike rocked Lawrence, Massachusetts, in 1912. Yet the social and political issues behind that strike—the acculturation of immigrants, the relationship of industrial workers to corporate employers, the authority of the state to regulate that relationship—reached beyond the borders of industrial New England in the first two decades of this century. Bootleggers in Chicago in the 1920s aped the organizational techniques of the businessmen-heroes of the Jazz Age; the nation's divisions over Prohibition showed in the city's ambivalence about gangsters. Auto workers in Detroit shared the prosperity of the 1920s, the hardship of the depression, the benefits of the New Deal, and the social dislocation of the Second World War. During the bus boycott in 1955–1956, blacks in Montgomery, Alabama, modestly disclaimed any special distinction; if they were the "new Negroes" journalists wanted to call them, then there were "new Negroes" all over the South. And the riots in Watts near Los Angeles ten years later foreshadowed an epidemic of urban violence.

None of these events would have occurred elsewhere in precisely the same way. The industrial legislation of Massachusetts in 1912 and the welfare regulations of California in 1965 shaped the strike in Lawrence and created discontent in Watts. The leadership of Al Capone in Chicago and of Martin Luther King, Jr., in Montgomery made an incalculable difference. The peculiarities of the automobile industry set Detroit apart from other industrial cities. Ethnic neighborhoods and regional traditions persist in Detroit and elsewhere. Climate, topography, dialect, and diet vary from place to place.

Yet the pace of cultural homogenization has quickened in the last few decades, and the characteristics that differentiate one part of the United States from another are less obvious than formerly. Geographic mobility has increased and the media of national communication have flooded areas that used to be back waters; camping trailers slow traffic through once deserted hills and hollows, and television brings the same message to the Back Bay in Boston and the barrios of Texas and California.

An enlarged role for the federal government has been both cause and result of this lessening regionalism. When local government received most of a citizen's tax dollar and supplied most public services, political arguments centered in town halls and county courthouses. But the federal income tax, federal courts, federal bureaucrats, and the services voters have asked the federal government to provide have combined to overshadow local politics. A local legislative body cannot effectively control a national corporation, prohibit racial discrimination or the sale of alcohol in neighboring communities, or defend the country from Nazis or Communists. So strings lead from Washington to every hamlet in the land.

And from other places as well. Corporate resolutions passed in Cleveland or San Francisco close factories in Missouri, reduce the income of longshoremen on three coasts, and force a housewife in Montana to drive fifteen additional miles to buy groceries. Union officials convene in Miami to fix wage scales for Seattle or to schedule a strike for St. Paul. Merchandisers in Chicago decide what eight-year-old children will wear to school, and network executives in Los Angeles or New York determine what will amuse them.

The perspective of ordinary Americans has not invariably grown with their enlarging world. An anxious debtor, worried about paying installment loans, does not give much thought to the nation's fiscal policy and the rediscount rate. Many voters still have a more definite opinion about the county's purchase of an air-conditioned police cruiser than about the Pentagon's contract for billion-dollar aircraft. Even in the midst of the Second World War, Americans at home cared more about jobs and rationing than about foreign affairs. Most people, in short, do not live on a national scale, but in a smaller, more comprehensible compass—family, factory, school, neighborhood. Or rather, they live on several scales at once.

A crisis collects the various dimensions of a community's life at one focus. The customs of an ethnic group, the policies of a corporation, the rights of local citizens, the practices of police, the ambitions of politicians, and the orders of distant courts—all may convert a small incident into a big crisis that helps set the nation's course. Intervention by the larger society, bearing writs or arms or money, has become increasingly likely as the century has progressed. The federal government investigated the working conditions of Lawrence's immigrants only after the strike was over. Most

3

of the task of enforcing Prohibition fell on local police, including those in Chicago. When Detroit's welfare budget fell short of providing for the unemployed in the depression, the federal government helped; when Detroit's police could not quell a race riot during the Second World War, federal troops restored order. A federal court's decree rescued Montgomery's boycotting blacks from legal jeopardy, and financial assistance from sympathizers outside the city maintained an alternative system of public transportation. In some measure, the violence in Watts and elsewhere during the 1960s was a conscious effort to capture the nation's attention and thus to influence national policy.

The catalytic effect of a crisis, indeed, means that the events in this book probably had more of an air of emergency than Americans who lived in the century sensed. Their crises were usually homely ones—too little money, too few automobiles, too much drink. The newspapers, to be sure, pointed to several larger crises every day, but readers usually shrugged them off as tangential to their lives. War swirled across North Africa, North Korea, and North Vietnam without creating an atmosphere of crisis at home until a son deserted or was hurt, or until the stores ran out of sugar and steak. The energy crisis, the environmental crisis, and the urban crisis have seemed the abstractions of future historians—important enough, no doubt, but lacking a personal dimension until lines formed at the gasoline pumps or the elevators failed to work. Even discrimination has been less a crisis than a constant fact of existence for racial and ethnic minorities.

Crises beget violence, and there is considerable violence in this book. A militant black man is supposed to have said that violence was as American as cherry pie, an insight that can be dismissed too complacently. The violence in these pages is open, dramatic, unusual. But violence can be so familiar as to be unremarked; exploitation, discrimination, and harsh words can become routine, with the countryside destroyed, a family ruined, and a personality scarred as a result. Americans tend to overlook everyday violence, think of themselves as peaceful, and invoke compromises, contracts, ordinances, and other devices to keep their communities calm. Even Al Capone wearied of violence, and the resigned tolerance of Chicago's crime-jaded citizens ran out.

Frequently, apologists alleged that a community's violence came from outside—from labor organizers, Communists, militants, and agitators. Civic spirit prohibited an admission that disorder might simply be an open form of the ritualized conflict between classes and races that had previously passed for social peace. This same defensive impulse protected policemen, who did not infallibly excel rioters either in discipline or in dedication to law and order. Perhaps placid policemen served placid communities, but some of those in the pages that follow aggravated the suppressed violence of the communities they served. Policemen personified as well as defended the status quo; they gave an unbending institutional expression to society's official orthodoxy and unofficial custom. Their conduct reflected not only their orders but the community's pressure—the subtle pressure of public opinion and the corrupting pressure of politics and property.

Reformers attempt to alleviate crises, to mediate between races and classes. The word "reformer" connotes disinterest; the readiness to grind another's axe gives the effort credibility. A physician's advocacy of factory regulations seems more objective and may have more weight than identical words from an industrial laborer. The middle-class proponent of larger welfare budgets seeks reform, while the welfare mother with the same objective seems ungrateful and greedy. Almost by definition, reformers are do-gooders who risk patronizing those they seek to help. Their detachment has sometimes produced reforms nobody needed, like Prohibition, or ones that missed the mark, like a reduction in working hours that brought an intolerable reduction in wages. Disinterest, in other words, has not guaranteed wisdom.

Nor have reformers acknowledged or always realized their own interest in social stability. They have advanced reform as a way of preventing more drastic change, a concession designed to preserve social harmony and the existing social order. Reformers insist that change flow through established legal and legislative channels and mesh with social custom. Government—the embodiment of law

5

and order—has been in the twentieth century a reformer's usual agent. Selection of that agent has placed political and constitutional limits on change and has guaranteed that reform would be gradual and follow familiar procedure.

Radicals, on the other hand, subordinate detachment, patience, and orderly process to the change they advocate. Radicals claim a comradeship with society's victims and a monopoly on morality that makes compromise immoral and opposition unjust. They deprecate governmental process as glacial and reform as an attempt to tame, and often to prevent, significant change. They believe that the oppressed themselves can compel an equitable division of society's benefits—in an orderly way if society be willing; by force if not.

A crisis tends to magnify the differences between radicals and reformers and to obscure the distaste of both for defenders of the status quo. In 1912, the Industrial Workers of the World wrote off the American Federation of Labor and progressive politicians as apologists for the woolen trust. Communists in Detroit during the depression argued that Henry Ford, Franklin Roosevelt, and the city's compassionate mayor all occupied the same leaking capitalist lifeboat. Because Martin Luther King, Jr., denounced violence and vandalism as well as bigotry, militant young blacks in Watts ridiculed him as an ally of profiteering storekeepers and racist cops. None of these accusations clarified the several possible methods of coping with strike, depression, or riot. Nor was any of them entirely false because, if driven to choose, reformers did ordinarily prefer stability to upheaval.

These examples magnify a detail on the canvas of the American past, where distinctions of person and place necessarily disappear. Historical synthesis blends (and often loses) the extreme, the unusual, and the local in a comprehensive version of the country's past that is not the past of anyone in it. The careful, abstract world of the national historian seems at once too complex and too simple: too complex because of its national scope, and too simple because it has lost the random disorder of life as people actually live it. A numerical average, however useful, may not accurately describe a column of numbers; an historical average, however true to an historian's data, may not be true to life.

Local history, on the other hand, has its own peculiar perspective. The apparent continuity of American communities, for instance, is deceptive, for people do not stay in one place even if their cities do. Local history necessarily focuses on a place, not on people, many of whom drift through an area without leaving a mark. A decennial census shows change in a city's total population, but not the thousands of changes that balance one another and do not affect the eventual total. Either because they have just arrived, or because they are about to depart, many residents of a twentieth-century American community have little identification with the turf they momentarily occupy. Local customs do not necessarily reflect their convictions, nor is local tradition their past.

Customs and conviction, crisis and violence, radicals and reformers, policemen, politicians, and the growing proximity of the federal government—these are the themes and the people of this book. The incidents of each chapter, diverse in time and place, illustrate some aspects of the twentieth-century American past. They do not themselves constitute a full history of that century or an inclusive interpretation of it. They do not in every case lead to a tidy conclusion, and in their inconclusiveness they denote both the complexity and the variety of the nation's recent history.

"I speak," the philosopher George Santayana once wrote, "of the American in the singular, as if there were not millions of them, north and south, east and west, of both sexes, of all ages, and of various races, professions, and religions." "Of course," Santayana continued, "the one American I speak of is mythical; but to speak in parables is inevitable in such a subject, and it is perhaps as well to do so frankly."[1]

This is a collection of parables.

Notes

[1] George Santayana, *Character and Opinion in the United States* (New York: C. Scribner's Sons, 1920), p. 167.

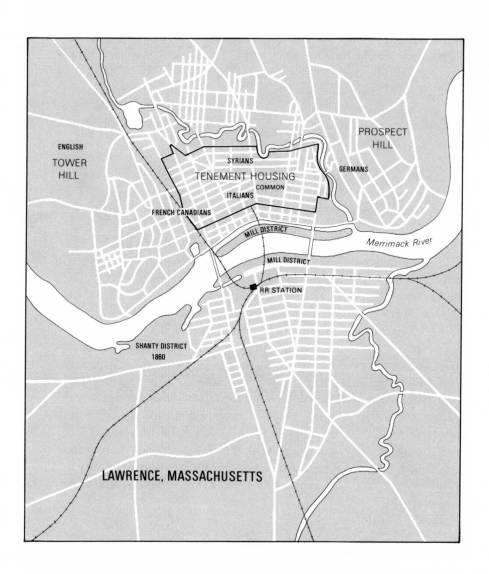

ENGLISH
TOWER
HILL

PROSPECT
HILL

SYRIANS

TENEMENT HOUSING
COMMON

GERMANS

ITALIANS

FRENCH CANADIANS

MILL DISTRICT

Merrimack River

MILL DISTRICT

RR STATION

SHANTY DISTRICT
1860

LAWRENCE, MASSACHUSETTS

"Not Enough Pay": 1
Lawrence, 1912

The looms stopped. An eerie stillness settled over the weaving room of the Everett Mill. News of the interruption reached the offices, where the staff was busy with the payroll for about 2000 employees. On an ordinary day, one man might have investigated. Thursday, January 11, 1912, was no ordinary day, and several officials, joined by an interpreter, made their way toward the weaving room. Through the interpreter, someone asked one of the weavers why she had shut down her machine. Using English instead of her usual Polish, the woman replied, "Not enough pay."

She was right on two counts: her envelope contained less money than she usually received, and, by most measures, even her usual wage was too low. One of the men explained that a new state law permitted women and children under eighteen to work no more than fifty-four weekly hours, two fewer than before. Surely, he went on, the weavers expected wages to fall in proportion. The woman heard him out, and repeated "Not enough pay."

The looms remained still. The managers concluded that a strike had begun and asked the idle weavers to leave the mill quietly. As they left, the weavers persuaded other workers to join them. When the mills closed on Thursday evening, a third of the looms lacked operators. On Friday morning, one in eight was in service. At noon on Saturday, the Everett Mill closed. That was only the beginning.

"AMERICA IN MICROCOSM"

"Lawrence, Massachusetts," one historian has written, "was America in microcosm" in the winter of 1912.[1] The mills that now seem dingy and brooding were new and throbbing then, symbols of the country's vigorous industrialization. The mixed accents and tongues that bubbled through tenements and factories illustrated the collision of "new" immigrants from southern and eastern Europe with northern Europeans who had arrived a generation or two earlier. In the city's suburbs and middle-class neighborhoods, concerned professional and business people worried about the potential political power of naturalized but unassimilated immi-

Mills in Lawrence

The Wood Mill

grants, about the exploitation of factory workers by corporate employers, about the social consequences of industrial and urban growth.

The strike held the nation's attention because other Americans had the same fears. The solidarity of Lawrence's ethnically diverse workers suggested the existence of social classes and the possibility of class warfare, developments that belied much national folklore. The glimpse of social and economic upheaval both enraged and terrified those with most to lose. Reformers understood, and to some extent shared, that reaction. But the strike also emphasized for them the necessity of enlightened change, the need for more tolerable working conditions and fairer wages. The apparent success of a radical labor union, which thrilled those opposed to capitalism, revealed to other Americans the weakness of ordinary labor organizations and the inadequacy of factory legislation already enacted. For a few months, Lawrence became a social laboratory, testing for a fascinated nation beliefs that had evolved in a simpler society.

Those beliefs were best expressed by people called progressives in the years before the First World War. The term "progressive" lacked

11

Inside the mills

precision and the "progressive movement" certainly was neither coherent nor unified. Indeed, most Americans subscribed to much of the progressive creed, which held that the American system, although fundamentally sound, could be improved through the careful effort of decent, disinterested people. Progressives tended to see most other Americans in their own image—as calm and reasonable citizens, more sympathetic to individualism and property rights than recent immigrants and laborers, less greedy and cynical than industrial oligarchs. It was a confident vision, sometimes condescending, but rarely arrogant or mean.

Nor was it entirely accurate. Industrialization seemed merely to alter the scale of things: factories replaced shops, cities grew from towns, proprietors became corporations, employees joined unions. But a qualitative change accompanied this change of scope. The tasks of city governments were not only greater than those of towns but were often entirely different tasks. Factories not only produced more shoes than had artisans, but converted shoemakers from craftsmen to unskilled "hands." Immigrants, who arrived in mounting numbers, differed in language, religion, tradition, and property from those who had come earlier.

Most progressives recognized the existence of social injustice, but they did not always correctly identify its causes. Often they explained social dislocation as the result of inefficiency or some local or individual "abuse," such as political corruption or monopolistic power. The most obvious evils were those closest to home— dishonest aldermen, noisome slums, high fares on streetcars. And the first line of defense was also local: better candidates, judicious pressure on landlords and employers, municipal regulation or even ownership of public services. The variety of the so-called progressive movement, and much of its vitality as well, reflected its origin in local circumstance. The smorgasbord of solutions reflected the diverse provisions of dozens of state constitutions and hundreds of municipal charters, as well as the interests of reformers themselves.

Two groups of Bay State reformers seemed rivals as often as allies. One was Yankee, patrician or middle-class, professional, Republican, Protestant, and personally tied to industry only through dividends. Cities and immigrants, as these progressives saw them, were part of the problem. The other progressive strain consisted of just the sort of people that made the first group apprehensive. City-dwellers, of Irish or more recent immigrant stock, Catholic, and often connected with labor unions and Democratic political machines, these urban liberals were developing a program that foreshadowed a half century of American reform.

Massachusetts reformers had enacted during the nineteenth century much of the legislation that engaged their counterparts elsewhere in the years before the First World War. The state's legislature established commissions to regulate railroads and public utilities, a bureau of labor statistics to permit informed industrial regulation, and incorporation laws that discouraged "trusts." Several Massachusetts communities experimented with municipal ownership of generating plants to supply power for street lights, and a few with municipal distribution of fuel and other consumer goods. The state had tried to restrict child labor as early as 1836, and subsequently provided for the inspection of factories to insure decent conditions and appropriate safety procedures. In 1874, ten hours became the legal working day for women and children; the maximum work week was reduced to fifty-eight hours, to fifty-six in 1910, and then to fifty-four, effective January 1, 1912.[2]

Ironically, that final reduction triggered the strike in Lawrence. Before 1912, most industrial managers had adjusted wages so that fewer hours had not caused thinner pay envelopes. The action was voluntary, because most judges agreed that states could not enact a minimum wage. In 1912, Lawrence's managers refused to discuss a compensatory raise, and anxious employees concluded that there would be none. On the first payday in January, then, the Polish weaver and her companions found "not enough pay." However pleasant the two weekly hours of additional leisure, she needed the money more.

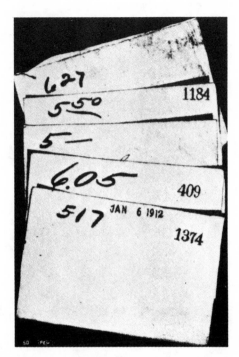

"Not enough pay"

After the strike began, in response to a resolution of the United States Senate, the Commissioner of Labor sent statisticians to Lawrence to find out where the money went. The strikers claimed their weekly wage averaged between $5 and $6, but Commissioner Charles P. Neill's careful figure was $8.76—about 15¢ or 16¢ an hour. The "full-time earnings of a large number of adult employees," Neill found, "are entirely inadequate to maintain a family." People apparently subsisted on bread (about 3¢ per loaf), beets and onions (a nickel per pound), potatoes (40¢ per peck), and cheap cuts of meat ("pork neck . . . 12¢"). Stew beef, eggs, and butter were luxuries.

The commissioner's investigators found that six families in ten took in lodgers to share the average $3 weekly rent; seven occupants in a four- or five-room flat seemed the usual census. Almost all of these dwellings had running water and toilets, but Lawrence's build-

15

Tenement housing

ing code did not regulate lighting, ventilation, or the structural adequacy of a building. In the wooden tenements of central Lawrence, Commissioner Neill observed, "the fire risk both to life and property is very great." Even without a fatal fire, long hours, congested living, and inadequate diet shortened lives. Textile cities, like Lawrence, had a notoriously high incidence of pneumonia and tuberculosis, and a notoriously high rate of infant mortality. The mean age at death in Lawrence was fifteen.[3]

At fifteen, many of Lawrence's residents had been at work for a year, and some for more than that. The state required attendance at school to age fourteen, a well-meant provision that both parents and employers too often had an interest in evading. Family income was so low that the few dollars a child earned could make the difference between eating and hunger. An inquiring congressman asked a boy

16

in 1912 whether he regretted his departure from school at the fourth grade and whether he wished the state had required him to attend until he was sixteen. Sure, the lad replied, and he continued with a question of his own: "but what would we eat?" At fifteen, his wages exceeded his father's; he was the oldest child and there were six others at home.[4]

Like most of Lawrence's inhabitants, the boy was the child of immigrants. Indeed most of the people in Massachusetts were either immigrants or the children of immigrants, though the foreign element in Lawrence was unusually large and diverse. Only 14 percent of the city's 85,000 inhabitants were native-born of native parents; almost half had been born abroad: nearly 8000 in Canada, most of whom spoke French as their native tongue; about 6500 in Italy; 6000 in Ireland; more than 4000 in parts of the Russian Empire, including Poland; and about 2000, called Syrians in Lawrence, who had been born in the Turkish Empire.[5]

THE FIRST DAYS

Formal delegations of employees ordinarily met a frosty reception in the offices of the Lawrence mills. Lest courtesy be mistaken for recognition of a labor organization, management routinely refused to answer questions from groups with any resemblance to a union. Late in 1911, when workers tried to discover how the fifty-four-hour law would be implemented, local managers turned them aside or referred them to corporate headquarters in Boston, whence no answer was forthcoming either. Lawrence officials reassured an executive from Boston, who asked whether a proportional reduction in wages would cause trouble: "At worst," they reported, a strike would "probably be confined . . . in a single mill."

Management, Commissioner Neill observed later, had lost touch with the people on the payroll. Posting the new law in the mills, as the law itself required, hardly constituted informing the employees and might be deliberately evasive, since Polish- and Italian-speaking workers could not reasonably be expected to understand legal English. Answering the questions of representative employees could

17

not, Neill thought, imply official recognition of a union; corporate refusal to talk with employees was a lame excuse for arrogance.[6]

William Madison Wood—behind his back people called him "Billy"—certainly thought he knew his employees. To be sure, he was the president of the American Woolen Company, the largest corporation in the business; as much as anyone, he was responsible for the mergers that built the hundred-million-dollar trust that owned the most important mills in Lawrence and employed several thousand people there. The orphaned son of a Portuguese sea cook, Wood himself had started work in a New Bedford textile mill when he was eleven. He worked hard, attracted the paternal interest of his employer, and moved up, and eventually on, to Lawrence where he married the boss's daughter. Wood always maintained that the interests of capital and labor coincided, and not even radicals doubted his sincerity. He believed he deserved the confidence of his employees, that he knew what was best for them. The workers would soon realize, he remarked at the outset of the strike in 1912, that "justice [was] not on their side," and that their action was "hasty and ill-advised." He was, Wood said, as much a corporate employee as they were.

> ... I am bound ... to take proper care of the interests of 13,000 stockholders [and] ... of some 25,000 employees. It is my duty to see that each side has a square deal.... I have consulted long and anxiously with the directors.... Reluctantly and regretfully we have come to the conclusion that it is impossible ... to grant any increase in wages.... I ask you to have confidence in this statement and to return to your work.... [F]our times this company has increased your wages without your asking.... This proves that I have looked after your interests pretty well in the past. Why should I not have your confidence for the future?[7]

There was, Joe Ettor thought, an answer to that question in the first sentence of the basic document of the Industrial Workers of the World (IWW): "The working class and the employing class have nothing in common." Like William Wood, Joe Ettor was the son of a working man; like Wood, Ettor had started early to make his own way. He drifted from Brooklyn to Chicago to San Francisco, where

William M. Wood

he learned a skilled trade, survived the 1906 earthquake, and watched the great fire with his friend the proletarian novelist Jack London. At seventeen Ettor sent his nickel to Socialist party headquarters to purchase a red button; in 1907, at twenty-two, he was in the logging camps of Oregon enrolling lumberjacks in the IWW. Soon he had a hand in the IWW's efforts to organize workers in steel mills, shoe shops, and mining camps.

Joe Ettor could deliver the union's simple message in English, Italian, Polish, Yiddish, and broken Hungarian. He told his audiences that one industrial union of skilled and unskilled, male and female, immigrant and native, was the only effective force against the united bosses. He called industrial sabotage a legitimate weapon in that no-holds-barred struggle. He damned private property as legal theft and the government as the agent of the exploiting class. Not for Joe Ettor the moderate's search for harmonious compromise; he had chosen the workers' side. The workers in Lawrence never thought of him as the outsider Wood tried to paint him when Ettor arrived in January 1912.

Organizing industrial workers was difficult because they had little bargaining power. The nation's major labor union, the American Federation of Labor (AFL), concentrated on craftsmen whose skills gave them an economic leverage that textile workers, for instance, lacked because unskilled labor abounded. Still, the AFL chartered a textile affiliate, the United Textile Workers (UTWU), and spent money, energy, and prestige in a futile drive in Lawrence, where in 1912 fewer than one in ten textile workers belonged to any labor organization. John Golden, president of the UTWU, attributed his union's failure to the presence of "these new people, unacquainted with our ways, unable to speak our language," who were willing to work for wages that would have outraged "English-speaking people. . . ." He told the congressional committee investigating the strike that "the Federal Government should seriously consider the restricting of immigration," an ironic stance for one who had himself immigrated about twenty years earlier. The workers in Lawrence displayed their own sense of irony in a booklet entitled *What John Golden Has Done for the Textile Workers;* bound inside the impressive cover were several eloquent blank pages.[8]

Even without a union, the strike quickly spread beyond the Everett Mill. Payday elsewhere in the city was Friday, January 12, and most employees expected less money than usual and more trouble. The worried paymaster at the Washington Mill delayed his rounds when he heard that knots of workers were collecting, talking instead of working. When disorder began, he suggested that Frank Sherman at the Wood Mill ought to secure the doors. Sherman moved too slowly. "Within three minutes," he said later, "I heard the most ungodly yelling and howling and blowing of horns I ever heard. . . ." The paymaster, "scared white," reported that the mob had come through the doors and overpowered the watchman. Sherman told the paymaster to lock up the cash and let the crowd run its

20

course until the police came. As they had done in the Washington Mill, strikers shut down machinery, by throwing the switch, by slashing the belt, or simply by pulling the operator into the throng that rushed on. Untended machines ruined some unfinished fabric, and the unruly crowds knocked over stacks of finished goods. Sherman waited until the wave subsided; it lasted about thirty minutes.[9]

Sherman's tactics foreshadowed management's approach to the strike: lock up the money, let the first spontaneous energy dissipate, send for the police, and distribute thin pay envelopes. While employers sat tight, disgruntled employees sought a method of converting the demonstration to a strike. A few members of the IWW—in more or less good standing—sent for Joe Ettor, who arrived on Saturday and used the weekend to devise an organizational structure that raised money, sustained morale, and kept the strikers united and the community on edge for almost two months. Ettor used the threat of violence, and the city's fear of it, to counter management's strategy of delay. He could not prevent every thrown rock and fist, but even an unfriendly observer noted that Ettor controlled the strikers "as completely as any general ever controlled his disciplined troops."[10]

Ettor's device was a strike committee organized by ethnic group, rather than by craft as the AFL would have done, or by mill or employer, a pattern the owners preferred. Each group elected three representatives, who typically assembled in the morning to receive reports ("The Syrians are standing firm"; "there are a few scabs among the Jews.") and to discuss plans. The representatives returned to their neighborhoods later in the day to carry instructions and to encourage the faint-hearted. Ettor presided, but the committee was not an arm of the IWW. It was the strike, not the union, that was important.

On Sunday, the newly formed committee agreed on a set of demands. Fifty-six-hours' pay for fifty-four-hours' work was no longer enough. The strikers asked an immediate 15 percent increase in wages and double pay for overtime. In addition, they demanded abolition of the "premium system," a schedule of monthly bonuses employers used to speed up production. To protect their jobs, strikers wanted management's promise not to discharge anyone because of activity during the strike. Significantly, they did not insist on recognition of their union. The committee encouraged workers to gather at the gates of the mills on Monday morning to persuade (or intimidate) those who might want to return to work.

That was the sort of activity Mayor John Scanlon intended to prevent. He called the city's commissioners into session at 5:45 on Saturday morning to provide more policemen for the emergency. He warned strikers against violence, asked that they not congregate in the streets, and suggested that they start negotiations with management promptly. He probably could not have done more. Mayor Scanlon had taken office only two weeks before under a new city charter that replaced politicians with commissioners. The new officials were supposed to be experts, capable of providing services more efficiently and less expensively than corruptible politicians. Progressives around the country advocated the city commission form of government partly to avoid the ethnic politics to which Lawrence was especially susceptible. But ethnic representatives, as Joe Ettor recognized, at least had standing in their neighborhoods, which "experts" sometimes lacked. And the experts in Lawrence, like the politicians they succeeded, all seemed to be Irish anyhow.

Mayor Scanlon took another step on Sunday with an order that sent one company of militia to the armory. He asked for two more on Monday morning, when police met pickets on the bridges leading to the mills. The crowd surged up the bridges, and harried officials turned on the fire hoses. Strikers parried with hunks of ice, coal, and other handy trash. Panic mounted inside the mills as windows smashed. About thirty strikers braved the barricades and the water and attempted to shut down the mill. Soldiers and police reinforcements arrived, scattered the crowd, and arrested thirty-six strikers. The city's courts acted promptly: within hours of their arrest, twenty-four rioters had been sentenced to a year in jail, and those carrying weapons received two years.

The mayor's attempt to promote negotiations foundered when management refused to meet with mediators. The strike committee did assemble and outlined the demands strikers had approved the

Fire hose holds strikers off

day before. But, William Wood said, employers had no counterpro-
posals for workers who destroyed property and were "in no frame of
mind to discuss conditions." The city's responsibility, Wood continued, was not to find a compromise, but to end "mob rule." Mayor
Scanlon had already sent for more soldiers.[11]

Scanlon's request went to Governor Eugene Foss, whose preelec-
tion record had contained little to cheer advocates of industrial
reform. Foss himself owned textile mills; his success as a businessman plus his ability to contribute heavily to Democratic campaigns
combined to bring him a slightly tainted nomination for governor in
1910. He won the election, reelection twice, and promised to run
the state "along well established business lines."

Eugene N. Foss

Yet once in office Foss was not the stereotypical probusiness executive. Instead he compiled a progressive record of the urban liberal stripe. Although he vetoed bills that permitted picketing, he signed other labor legislation, including the fifty-four-hour law, which he did not like, and a first attempt to establish workman's compensation. He approved statutes that regulated railroad rates, monopolistic prices, and tenement housing. It was sober legislation, offering more to organized labor than unions had had before, and annoying "the interests" without undermining them. The Foss administration, in short, encouraged a somewhat more democratic and humane society, but did not fundamentally challenge the existing social order.[12]

The governor sent troops to Lawrence, and his secretary, Dudley Holman, as well. Foss wanted a first-hand report and, if possible, a resolution of the strike before events slipped out of control. Holman met late Monday night with Mayor Scanlon, police officials, and Colonel Leroy Sweetser, the officer in charge of the militia. Early the next morning, Holman prowled the mill district looking for Ettor, whose office seemed to be in the streets. Accompanied at first by Ettor's self-appointed bodyguards, who feared he might be arrested, the two men walked and talked in the subzero dawn. Holman reported the governor's hope that the state board of arbitration might be helpful. Ettor did not like the idea, but presented it to the strike committee, where a majority overruled him. Holman telephoned Foss to convey the strikers' willingness to take their case to the state agency.

The meeting never took place. The strikers sent the delegation they had promised. The state board of arbitration appeared. But several employers, including American Woolen, refused to send representatives. Consequently, Holman said, "the thing fell through." A committee of the Massachusetts legislature subsequently held an equally barren session in Lawrence. Two weeks later, Foss himself sought a way out of the impasse. He asked the workers to return to the mills for thirty days, and he asked the employers to keep weekly wages at the fifty-six-hour level. A month, Foss thought, should suffice for him to find a solution. He pledged his "best efforts" and expected "a settlement satisfactory to all parties." Nobody answered his letter.[13]

VICTORY!

The strike in Lawrence began about six weeks after James McNamara had ended a sensational trial by pleading guilty to blowing up the headquarters of the *Los Angeles Times* in the course of labor warfare in southern California. For some time after that explosion, any American labor dispute inspired rumors of dynamite. Stories flashed through Lawrence and surfaced in the press—prematurely in one instance when a Boston newspaper described a cache police located about the time the headline appeared. Checking reports of three other bombs, Lawrence police raided a tenement in the Syrian district, where they found some explosives and arrested seven residents. More dynamite turned up in the cobbler shop in the Italian district Joe Ettor used as an address; the cobbler was arrested. But the police had trouble with the third batch they had heard about, which was supposed to be somewhere near the cemetery.

Who knew more about Lawrence's cemeteries than John Breen, the genial undertaker who had first told the police about the dynamite? Breen drew a map for the officers, who returned to the cemetery and found what they were looking for. It seemed a little strange that the explosives were wrapped in an undertaker's trade journal; it seemed even more strange when police discovered that only Breen, of all the city's undertakers, did not have that issue. The judge at the local police court, who without hesitation had sentenced "rioters" to a year, threw out the cases against the Syrians and the cobbler.

Cobbler and shop where dynamite was discovered

Persons "interested in maintaining a reign of terror in this city," said Judge J. J. Mahoney, not the immigrant defendants in his courtroom, had planted the dynamite.

As a matter of fact—and of increasingly common knowledge—John Breen had. A local contractor, showing the effect of too much drink and perhaps of a troubled conscience as well, blurted to the prosecuting attorney that William Wood had had his hands on the dynamite. Or at least that was the story the prosecutor told to a grand jury. But the contractor sobered up and killed himself, and the indictment of Wood did not stick. Breen was convicted, fined, and recalled from the school committee, which was supposed to have been the first step toward succeeding his father as the city's Irish political boss.

The bungled dynamite plot was only one indication of rising tension as the days became weeks and neither side flinched. The strike committee improved its organization by adding alternates and designating substitutes to take over if leaders were arrested. A major effort to raise funds among radicals and labor groups brought in nearly $1000 each day to provide soup kitchens and living allowances for strikers and their families. Ettor designed new tactics to make picketing more effective and to harass the inexperienced militiamen. Parading pickets carried the American flag, taunted the soldiers to salute it, and then pushed through the formation that was supposed to be a barrier, shouting, "The American flag can go anywhere." Women—pregnant women if possible—marched in the first ranks of the strikers' demonstrations in order to make security forces think twice about nightsticks and bayonets. Other women, when arrested, refused to post bond or otherwise to expedite trial, and then nursed and cared for their children while in jail. When authorities forbade pickets to stop and talk with employees willing to return to work, Ettor marshaled 10,000 strikers who moved continuously through the mill district, thereby complying with the order and defeating its purpose. Pickets linked arms and swept singing through the streets four- or five-abreast. When police or militia disrupted the columns, large groups, still singing and still with linked arms, moved from the streets to the stores. Nervous customers departed and nervous merchants protested. A congressman subsequently asked the acting chief of police why he had not arrested the leaders of these demonstrations. "There are no leaders in the streets," the bewildered chief replied.[14]

Monday, January 29, started badly when strikers stopped streetcars in order to keep passengers from reaching the mills. By seven in the morning, derailed cars, broken windows, and bruised patrons persuaded managers of the street railway company to shut the line down. The crowd, its anger momentarily dampened, flowed off singing radical songs. Several thousand jeering strikers paused in

Strikers confront militia

Grave of Annie LoPezzi

front of the residence of a priest who had urged his flock to return to work. People loudly discussed demolition of church and rectory, and then the throng moved along. When the bayonets of militiamen blocked further progress, Ettor tactfully diverted the demonstrators up a side street to avoid confrontation, for the mood of the city became increasingly ugly as the day wore on.

That afternoon strikers and police clashed in one of the residential neighborhoods. The jostling ended in shots, and a young striker named Annie LoPezzi died on the sidewalk. Strikers claimed a police officer fired the fatal shot; the police alleged that someone shooting at an officer had accidentally killed a bystander instead. Joe Ettor and Arturo Giovannitti, the radical editor and poet who had accompanied Ettor to Lawrence, were arrested the following day, charged with having incited an unknown killer. Both men had been in other parts of the city when the shooting took place, but they were denied bail and remained in prison for the next ten months.[15] The strike committee added a new demand to the list: Ettor and Giovannitti must be released.

Murder inspired a formal resolution from the city council asking the militia to restore order. Governor Foss raised the available force to 1300 men by sending twelve additional companies of infantry and two troops of cavalry to Lawrence. Colonel Sweetser forbade meetings, parades, picketing, and intimidation, and stationed his troops all over the city. The next day, a detachment responded to a report that a parade was forming in the Syrian section. Troops moved to

The cavalry clears the streets after Annie LoPezzi's funeral

STRIKE TO FREE
ETTOR & GIOVANNITTI
IF THE CAPITALIST COURT CONVICTS THEM

TIE UP THE INDUSTRIES

TIE UP THE COUNTRY

The Real Accessories Before The Fact To Murder Are The TEXTILE CAPITALISTS And DYNAMITE PLANTERS.

THE VITAL STATISTICS OF LAWRENCE, MASS., SHOW THAT
The Average Length Of Life Of Its Manufacturers Is **58 YEARS**
The Average Length Of Life Of Its Textile Operatives Is **39 YEARS**
The Manufacturers of Lawrence live on an average 19 years longer than do the Workers who produce all the wealth.

Joe Ettor and Arturo Giovannitti

disperse the band. John Ramy, a young musician, did not move quickly enough and died of a bayonet wound in the back. There was a perfunctory investigation that disclosed no names. A congressman later remarked sarcastically that he had missed in the account of Lawrence's chief of police "what sort of deadly weapon the boy had in his hand at the time he was killed." "I did not say he had a deadly weapon," the chief replied; "I said he had a musical instrument."[16]

Colonel Sweetser had made his point. The strikers stayed at home. So did many of those whom the strikers had been intimidating. Unions representing skilled workers decided they were on strike too. In the second month of the strike the number of employees actually present in the mills dipped to its lowest point. A

31

A PROCLAMATION !

IS MASSACHUSETTS IN AMERICA ?

Ready to plunge the bayonets into woman's blood.

Military Law Declared in Massachusetts !
Habeas Corpus Denied in Massachusetts !
Free Speech Throttled in Massachusetts !
Free Assemblage Outlawed in Massachusetts !
Unlawful Seizure of Persons in Massachusetts !
Unwarranted Search of Homes in Massachusetts !
Right to Bear Arms Questioned in Massachusetts !
Mill Owners Resort to Dynamite Plots and Violence in Massachusetts!

Militia Hired to Break Strike in Massachusetts !
Innocent People Killed by Militia in Massachusetts!
Militia Ordered to Shoot to Kill in Mass. !

Unusual Bail and Fines Exacted in Massachusetts!
Corporations Control Administrations in Mass. !

The striking textile workers of Lawrence, Massachusetts are confronted with the above described conditions. They are making a noble fight for an increase of wages and to prevent discriminations against the members of the organization carrying on this strike. To abolish a pernicious premium system inaugurated for no other purpose than the speeding up of already overworked toilers. If you want to assist the strikers send funds to JOSEPH BEDARD, 9 Mason Street, Franco-Belgian Hall, Financial Secretary Textile Workers Industrial Union, Lawrence, Massachusetts.

reporter visited the Washington Mill, where the machinery hummed. But, he noted, "not a single operative was at work and not a single machine carried a spool of yarn."[17] His visit verified Big Bill Haywood's remark that "You can't weave cloth with bayonets."

Members of the IWW were often called "wobblies" and one-eyed William D. (Big Bill) Haywood had a national reputation as the wildest "wobbly" of them all. His foes, and some of his radical comrades, exaggerated Haywood's penchant for violence, but he was indeed a charismatic man with a genuine outrage about the exploitation of industrial workers and a demonstrated ability to inspire them. After Ettor's arrest, Haywood replaced him on the strike committee and assumed much of the responsibility for directing the strike. Together with Elizabeth Gurley Flynn, the twenty-two-year-old "red flame," and others of the union's hierarchy, he whipped up the spirit of workers on the scene and raised money outside the city for their support.

An Italian immigrant at a meeting in New York City did not have much money. But his family, he said, would welcome a child or two from a striker's family. Although one or two more mouths at his table would not make much difference, the absence of hungry babies might stiffen the resistance of wavering workers in Lawrence. That was how workers in the old country helped one another. Haywood and the strike committee liked the idea. *The Call*, a socialist daily in New York, made an appeal on behalf of "the little children of Lawrence," and volunteers appeared from all over the city.[18]

Other radicals in other places wanted their share of the heroic "little children." Emotional departures from the train station in Lawrence triggered one set of news releases, greetings at host cities

William Haywood speaks on the Lawrence Common

Elizabeth Gurley Flynn and Haywood with strikers' children

"The Little Children"

another. Physicians examined the children and gave out statements about rickets and malnutrition. Observers remarked the shabby clothing children wore and the paradoxical fact that those who wove woolen cloth could not afford to wear it. Margaret Sanger, an idealistic young nurse whose experience in public health would make her the nation's foremost proponent of birth control, testified that only 4 of the 119 children she examined wore underwear.[19]

As the children moved out, the money rolled in, and the strike dragged on. The Lawrence city fathers, proud of their city, thought it deserved better than the publicity the "little children" generated, and decided to keep them at home. Colonel Sweetser informed the strike committee that he would not "permit the shipping off of little children . . . unless I am satisfied that this is done with the consent of their parents."[20]

Within a few days, the strike committee announced that 150 children would, with the consent of their parents, accept invitations to visit Philadelphia for the duration of the strike. On the day of departure, almost two months after the walkout began, early arrivals at the depot noticed a company of militia parading in the street outside. Inside, an inordinate number of policemen fanned out through the station, clearing out loiterers and then assembling in two parallel ranks leading toward a door. Outside the door, the chief had parked an open truck he had borrowed from the militia. He approached the children, who had clustered in the waiting room, and told them of the city's readiness to supply charitable relief: "[I]f any of you make a . . . request for aid or assistance you will receive it." Only about 40 children, and fewer adults, had withstood the intimidating show of force, and they were not deterred by the chief's kind words. They declined to argue, waited for the train, and moved to board it when it was announced. The police diverted them to the truck, and thence to jail.

Waiting for the children at the depot

But not without an uproar. The radical press described beatings, blood, miscarriages, and weeping, bruised children in cells. The rhetoric was borrowed from Russian uprisings—Cossacks, tyranny, pogroms. Even Samuel Gompers, the president of the AFL and no supporter of the tactics of the IWW, grumbled that nobody would have detained the sons and daughters of millionaires. Judge Ben Lindsay, a reformer from Denver known as "the children's judge," noted that "those children will probably not miss the Constitution—they have missed so much else." The Attorney General of the United States said the authorities had made "a stupid blunder." Months later, the police chief was still bewildered. He had not seen any violence, he said; he was just enforcing the statute that prohibited parental neglect of children.[21]

One of the congressmen investigating the strike was delighted at last to have a statute to discuss. He tried to pin down the chief's superior, Lawrence's Commissioner of Public Safety: "Under what law of the State of Massachusetts were you acting in the matter?" The commissioner did not know "offhand." The congressman kept at it: "Did you know what the law was at the time?" The commissioner said somebody had looked it up. The congressman tried once more: Was there any applicable statute, he asked. "I think there is," was the best the commissioner could do. "Did you read that law?" the congressman inquired. "I did not read it; no sir," the commissioner replied. "I think not," the exasperated congressman remarked, and turned to another topic.[22]

Mill officials knew immediately that the scene at the station disgraced the one-sided law enforcement upon which they relied. They authorized a defensive statement denying responsibility for the city's effort to detain the children. "The manufacturers did not ask for this [action]; they were not consulted about it; they were not informed of the contemplated action of the local authorities."[23] The owners knew they were in trouble; the struggle could no longer be kept in Lawrence where they had a chance to control it. The Senate would soon send Commissioner Neill's investigators to Lawrence; the Committee on Rules of the House of Representatives convened hearings on the strike. Congressional criticism of the industry's

"Law and Order in Lawrence"

labor practices might undermine support for the textile schedules of the protective tariff.

And by the end of February, Governor Foss had had enough too. His disclaimer about events at the station echoed that of the mill owners: local authorities controlled the police; he had not been consulted; the militia was not involved. Indeed, Foss wrote the owners, it was time to send the militia home; he did not propose to have the military forces of Massachusetts used to break the strike. Both the governor and the owners knew that the militia's departure would leave discredited police officials responsible for law and order. Foss asked the state's attorney general to look into the incident at the depot to see whether any citizen's constitutional rights had been abridged. Foss then let the pressure build with the word that he was "disappointed" that management had not tried more diligently to settle the strike.[24]

In fact management had begun to seek a settlement, less because of political pressure than because of a flood of orders. On March 1, Wood met a delegation from the strike committee. American

37

Woolen would raise wages 5 percent, he said, and similar notices appeared in the other mills. The strikers thought Wood's offer too little, too late, and too vague. Within a week, the delegation had another invitation. It would take time, Wood said, to spell out the new rates for each employee. The strikers replied that they could wait until the lists were prepared, even though some of the skilled employees had already accepted Wood's terms. On March 9, Wood clarified his offer another time, with a schedule that showed a raise up to 11 percent. The strikers waited again. Three days later, Wood gave in: the raise for the most poorly paid workers was more than 20 percent, and no one received less than 5; an additional 25 percent would be paid for overtime. Premiums would be calculated every two weeks instead of once a month. No worker would be penalized for participation in the strike. The strikers met on the Lawrence Common, cheered, sang, and accepted.[25]

One troubling loose end remained: Ettor and Giovannitti were still in jail. The employers promised to use their influence to achieve the prisoners' release, but Essex County's legal staff stubbornly did its duty. Spring became summer, and summer turned to fall. Haywood and Flynn went on to other struggles in other cities, where they occasionally took up a collection to help pay their comrades' legal expenses. Roland Sawyer, a socially conscious minister from Ware and the Socialist party's candidate for governor against Eugene Foss, subordinated his political campaign to an effort to reach the jurors who might judge Ettor and Giovannitti. Sawyer made a batch of slides from his photographs of the strike, prepared a set of resolutions, and wrote an all-purpose speech, which he gave wherever he could find an audience.

Joe Ettor knew who his friends were. He sent Sawyer a warm note, thanking him for his public effort and private encouragement. Tell everybody for me, Ettor wrote, that "I am putting my time to good use reading and studying," that I "am enjoying my usual good health," that I "am not discouraged, [but] buoyant as ever." He was, Ettor claimed, guilty only of his *"loyalty to the working class."* If he were convicted, "and if the reward be death," he wrote, "I will part with life with a song on my lips."[26]

There was no need for that. The jury acquitted Ettor and Giovannitti and ended their months of imprisonment. The verdict came at Thanksgiving time, and there was indeed much to be thankful for. Textile workers elsewhere in New England received wage increases comparable to those in Lawrence, often without more than mentioning a strike. New windows and new belts made the mills as good as new, and the confidence of employers returned when membership in the IWW shrank as quickly as once it had grown. Civic boosters mounted a parade for "God and Country" to dramatize the transience of radicalism and the permanence of conventional values, and to restore the city's morale and public reputation.

Anxiety about Lawrence's reputation stemmed from intense national interest in the strike. Social workers, labor leaders, journalists, politicians, and miscellaneous tourists swarmed to the city to see events at first-hand. Senator Miles Poindexter of Washington, barred by police from interviewing those arrested at the railway station, told reporters the city was a "concentration camp." William Allen White, whose Emporia, Kansas, newspaper had a national circulation, remarked that the immigrant strikers possessed a

Polishing the city's image
after the strike

Essex County Jail and House of Correction

. . . .

Lawrence, Mass., _June_ 191 2

Rev. Roland D. Sawyer
    Ware, Mass.

Comrade:

Attorney Rowen brought me the
inscribed copy of your brochure,
also conveyed to me contents of your
note, many thanks for the book and
for kind words of support.

You ask me what message you
can give the workers in my name;

Assure all the sons and daughters of
toil of my absolute innocence on all
counts except loyalty to the working
class and if the reward be death I will
part with life with a song on my lips.

I assure you and all that I am
putting my time here to good use reading
and studying— am enjoying my usual
good health, have been unable to yet
acquire prison color, am as usual, but
strapped. But remember comrade,
am not discouraged, buoyant as ever,
only anxiety is to get back among the workers
as before & militant in the ranks
in the struggle for a better day.

The bard of Avon puts these words in Cassius mouth:

"Therein, ye gods, you make the weak most strong;
Therein, ye gods, you tyrants do defeat:
Nor stony tower, nor walls of beaten brass,
Nor airless dungeon, nor strong links of iron,
Can be retentive to the strength of the spirit."

With personal Salutations I am,
yours for the Cause

Geo. J. Etton

Reverend
Roland D. Sawyer
Ware, Mass.

"clearer vision of what America stands for than did many of those who sneered at them."[27] When Congressman Victor Berger, a Socialist from Milwaukee, introduced a resolution authorizing a congressional investigation, he submitted a sheaf of supportive petitions. They came from labor organizations in Mattoon, Illinois, and Moundsville, West Virginia; from Bellingham, Washington, and Bellefontaine, Ohio; from the city council of Thief River Falls, Minnesota, and the Socialists of Jersey City; from reformers in Spokane, Washington, and Washington, D.C.[28]

The strike caught the nation's attention because it offered a glimpse of what might be the future—a sobering preview for progressive, middle-class Americans, a shocking one for conservatives, and an exhilarating one for radicals and factory workers. To be sure, Lawrence was a unique community, and conditions there did not obtain in every other industrial center. But conditions might rapidly change: if immigration were not restricted, if wealth were not more equitably distributed, if unions and bosses were not restrained—if somebody, in short, did not do something—any place might become a Lawrence in the none-too-distant future.

That was no pleasant prospect—for progressives, in many ways, least pleasant of all. Through reform, they had intended to enable Americans to avoid precisely the sort of class confrontation that had manifestly occurred in Lawrence. Progressives hoped to convince employers that justice and self-interest alike demanded decent wages and working conditions. And progressives believed that those concessions, whether coerced by legislation or freely offered by enlightened businessmen, ought to persuade employees that the American system worked. Progressives advocated reform because they believed the nation's institutions were fundamentally fair. The strike in Lawrence suggested that reformers might have to choose between their acceptance of social stability and their sympathy for the victims of social injustice.

Walter Weyl, a journalist and student of labor disputes, continued to postpone the choice. As he surveyed the strike for *The Outlook*, a progressive weekly that carried Theodore Roosevelt's name on the masthead, Weyl favored both the strikers and the militia—well-behaved lads, Weyl thought, who ought to have been playing ball. He condemned radical labor leaders, particularly Ettor and Haywood, and also "ruthless, immoral, ill-advised" employers for creating an explosive situation: "If out of this caldron of disillusion there should come a quick, hot flame of violence, it must be promptly extinguished. *Neither may we allow men, however wealthy or respectable, to scatter explosives on the ground.*"[29]

In condemning impartially all parties to an industrial dispute, progressives often unconsciously paraded their own purity of motive. The "best citizens" of Lawrence—"judges, ministers, . . . bankers, shopkeepers, and workingmen of character and reputation," *The Outlook* reported—had begun a disinterested search for compromise. These people, "who are viewed with confidence by all classes," the editorial continued, should urge "operators to return to work at once."[30] And that, presumably, would be that. In the public interest, workers and owners alike ought to defer to middle-class citizens. The proposition was not necessarily wrong, but it had no connection with the behavior of real people in Lawrence, Massachusetts, or much of anywhere else.

Yet the people who faced Eugene Foss were real enough, as were those during other industrial disputes who visited other progressive mayors, governors, and Presidents. In difficult circumstances, Foss struck a progressive balance with more skill than contemporaries saw: he sent troops to restore order and prepared to withdraw them when their presence enhanced unduly the bargaining power of the mill owners. In other circumstances, other progressive politicians had to find a similar balance between order and justice, between the rights of employees and those of employers, between the need for governmental regulation and the tradition of individual liberty, between the protection of existing interests and the preservation of opportunity in the future.

That balance became increasingly elusive in the years before the First World War, and the optimistic faith of progressives increasingly difficult to sustain. In Lawrence, employers showed no shame about their unawakened social consciences, and employees spurned progressive remedies in favor of unions and radicalism and solutions

43

they designed themselves. Even progressive legislation, administered by progressive executives, had unpredictable, and sometimes
unprogressive, results. Had the fifty-four-hour law improved life in
Lawrence? If the commissioners enacted a new building code, would
mill workers be able to secure better housing? If William Wood were
converted to welfare capitalism, would the stockholders of American Woolen indulge him? Did it all come down to restricting immigration, as labor leaders and patricians alike suggested, or to Prohibition, which became the crusade of Governor Foss? Was that the best
the nation could do in the face of manifest injustice in Lawrence?

Walter Weyl kept coming back to a meeting in Mayor Scanlon's
office. The visiting state legislators were seeking a middle ground
and trying to impress the strikers with their good intentions and
good will. Finally one of the strikers asked the legislators just how
far they would go:

> If you find one party wrong, can your state force it to do right? . . .
> Would you arbitrate a question of life and death, and are the worst
> wages paid in these mills anything short of death? Do you investigate
> because conditions are bad, or because the workers broke loose and
> struck? Why did you not come before the strike? What can your state of
> Massachusetts do to make wrong right for the workingmen who are
> the bulk of your citizens?

That last one was the central question, Weyl thought. "What can
the state do? What can we do to make wrong right for the people of
our mills and factories?"[31] That was the question the strike had
posed. And the nation had, as yet, no certain answer.

Notes

[1]Melvyn Dubofsky, *We Shall Be All* (New York: Quadrangle, 1974), p. 235.

[2]Richard M. Abrams, *Conservatism in a Progressive Era* (Cambridge: Harvard University Press, 1964), *passim,* especially chapter 1.

[3]The report of the Commissioner of Labor was published as U.S., Congress, Senate,
Report on Strike of Textile Workers in Lawrence, Mass. in 1912, 62nd Cong., 2d sess.,
1912, Senate Document 870. The references in these paragraphs may be found at
pages 20, 486, and 27. See also Donald B. Cole, *Immigrant City* (Chapel Hill:
University of North Carolina Press, 1963), p. 212.

[4]U.S., Congress, House, Committee on Rules, *The Strike at Lawrence, Mass., Hearings Before the Committee on Rules . . . 1912*, 62nd Cong., 2d sess., 1912, House Document 671, p. 153.

[5]Cole, *Immigrant City*, p. 209.

[6]Senate Document 870, pp. 10–11.

[7]*Ibid.*, p. 40; see also John B. McPherson, *The Lawrence Strike of 1912* (Boston: The Rockwell and Churchill Press, 1912), p. 15.

[8]House Document 671, p. 81; see also Henry F. Bedford, *The Socialists and the Workers in Massachusetts, 1886–1912* (Amherst: University of Massachusetts Press, 1966), p. 248.

[9]House Document 671, pp. 439–40.

[10]McPherson, *Lawrence Strike*, p. 9.

[11]*New York Call*, January 16, 1912; Senate Document 870, pp. 37–38, 60.

[12]Abrams, *Conservatism in a Progressive Era*, pp. 251–61.

[13]House Document 671, 347–48, 350; Senate Document 870, p. 44.

[14]House Document 671, pp. 261ff, 292, 302; Philip S. Foner, *The Industrial Workers of the World* (New York: International Publishing Co., 1965), pp. 321–22.

[15]House Document 671, pp. 290–94; McPherson, *Lawrence Strike*, pp. 26–27; *New York Call*, January 29, 30, 1912.

[16]House Document 671, p. 296; Foner, *IWW*, p. 331; Senate Document 870, pp. 44–45.

[17]*New York Times*, February 1, 1912.

[18]*New York Call*, February 8–11, 1912.

[19]*Ibid.*, February 12, 1912; House Document 671, pp. 232–33.

[20]Senate Document 870, p. 51.

[21]*New York Call*, February 25, 29, 1912; House Document 671, pp. 303–09.

[22]House Document 671, p. 281.

[23]McPherson, *Lawrence Strike*, pp. 37–38; *New York Call*, February 29, 1912.

[24]*New York Call*, February 9, 1912; Foner, *IWW*, p. 341.

[25]Senate Document 870, pp. 54–59.

[26]Joe Ettor to Roland D. Sawyer, June 1912, ms in possession of author.

[27]*New York Call*, February 27, March 1, 1912.

[28]House Document 671, pp. 11–23.

[29]The italics are Weyl's; the reference is not literally to dynamite, but to social explosives. Walter Weyl, "The Strikers at Lawrence," in *Outlook*, February 10, 1912, pp. 309, 312.

[30]*The Outlook*, February 17, 1912, pp. 352, 353, 358.

[31]Weyl, pp. 311-312.

Federal agents pour beer into Lake Michigan

The Booze Business: 2
Chicago in the 1920s

Robert St. John remembered Chicago with his nose. The memory was unpleasant. Yet urban odors deter ambitious young men less than eight-year-old schoolboys, which St. John had been when his family moved to suburban Oak Park. So, after the Navy and a few months of college, holding his nose and seeking a job on one of the city's newspapers, Robert St. John returned to Chicago. It was, he thought, the right place to be at the time: "Every era in American history," he wrote later, "has been symbolized by a city." In the ebullient 1920s, it was Chicago's turn.

St. John rediscovered Chicago's slums and squalor and smells. He also felt the throbbing civic confidence that led the *Tribune* to proclaim itself "The World's Greatest Newspaper," and the city to boast in its motto "I will." "Chicago in the twenties felt she could do anything," St. John recalled, from supplying the nation's bacon to providing the best in grand opera. "Two-fisted and rowdy . . . vibrant and violent, impatient with those either physically or intellectually timid," Chicago was "youth's city" at a time of "flaming youth." He risked rhetorical overkill as he ran down the symbols of the decade:

> ... Chicago personified ... the ... *This Side of Paradise* era of hip flasks, flat chested girls, speakeasies, modernistic furniture, cubism, banged-haired female intellectuals, the streamlined Model-A Ford, rum-runners, gang wars, fast motor-cars, hell's the limit, one more for the road.[1]

St. John's list skimmed the surface. He did not sense the disillusionment that became a major theme of his Oak Park acquaintance, the novelist Ernest Hemingway, and other intellectuals. St. John did not mention the changes in public communication that, as a reporter, he must have encountered every day—the advertising, the radio, the national distribution of motion pictures. He did not allude to the stock-market obsession at decade's end, nor to the long-run economic developments that the crash interrupted. Perhaps he intended automobiles to stand for all consumer goods, but he might have included refrigerators and a hundred other electrical gadgets that illustrated the nation's rising standard of living. In his collection of clichés, he missed President Calvin Coolidge's aphorism that America's business was business.

The business that did recur on St. John's list was illicit: the booze business. The Eighteenth Amendment to the Constitution, ratified in 1919, prohibited "the manufacture, sale, or transportation of intoxicating liquors." Neither the amendment nor the later Volstead Act outlawed the consumption of alcohol; Prohibition did not make thirst criminal—only the production and distribution of intoxicating fluid to quench it. The Volstead Act, passed over President Woodrow Wilson's veto, defined "intoxicating liquors" as those containing one-half of 1 percent or more alcohol by volume, a proportion somewhat lower than the alcoholic content of sauerkraut. Congress also established controls for medicinal, sacramental, and industrial uses of alcohol, and exempted from the ban the fermentation of fruit juice at home for personal use.

The Volstead Act handed a billion-dollar business to criminals. In 1915, the production of beer, wine, and spirits had ranked fifth

"Uncle Sam's Home-Brew"

among the nation's industries in the amount of invested capital. The enactment of Prohibition created a nationwide opportunity for enterprising smugglers and gangsters. Bootlegging rapidly developed as a growth industry, one of several that flourished in the 1920s by providing prosperous Americans with consumer goods.

There were, of course, important differences between supplying illegal liquor and producing automobiles or radios or motion pictures. Successful legitimate businesses, for example, perfected new managerial and marketing techniques and systematically encouraged technological innovation. Corporate research laboratories pro-

Home distilling kits confiscated in Chicago

duced the refinements that sustained annual model changes; national advertising and installment credit provided new customers. Those new customers, and the new products they bought, fueled the decade's economic boom.

Sales, on the other hand, were less a problem for bootleggers than production. Their entrepreneurial devices and competitive practices, in consequence, resembled those of an earlier generation of industrialists more than those of the salesmen of the 1920s. Rum-running, in addition, posed unusual business risks. A bootlegging executive could not ordinarily rely on police to secure his shipments and warehouses, nor could he expect courts to enforce his contracts. Most booze merchants had to do without the protection of bonds on their employees, credit at the local bank, and conventional insurance. Competition frequently required firearms, as did protection of property, collection of accounts, and settlement of labor disputes. Yet the number of eager customers and the enormous potential profit made fines and prison, and even the chance of violent death, acceptable business conditions.

Supporters of the Volstead Act thought a modest appropriation would suffice for enforcement; Congress provided $2 million as a start. One senator thought $50 million would be more realistic, but Wayne Wheeler, the most effective lobbyist for the Anti-Saloon League (ASL), scoffed at that prediction. Although $50 million would not be too much to accomplish the Volstead Act's high purpose, Wheeler said, $5 million would do the job. State governments too underestimated the expense of enforcement. They raised more money to carry out hunting and fishing regulations than to enforce Prohibition. The miscalculation, absurd in retrospect, illustrates not only the naiveté of the drys, but their earnest, almost euphoric, idealism.

Not every dry was an idealist. As brewers and distillers supported the wets, so soft-drink manufacturers helped the drys. Some Southern whites wanted to deny blacks the alcohol that might dissolve their inhibitions. A few prudes thought all pleasure sinful except the pleasure they themselves derived from depriving others of bottled joy. Defenders of an ethic associated with John Calvin, the farm, and the past, identified drink with Catholicism, the city, and decadence. Such a movement was vulnerable to caricature, and Carry Nation, with her hatchet and her multiple frustrations, has since come to personify the crackpot crusade.

But a great many sane and ordinary citizens also voted to outlaw the saloon. They came disproportionally from south of the Mason-Dixon line and west of the Mississippi River—from small towns and farms, from evangelical Protestant churches, from old American white stock, from the middle classes. These groups differed temperamentally and had in the past divided politically. But they united against the liquor trust, the barroom, the political machines and their bosses, urban immigrants, and a new morality that seemed to be oozing from the cities and threatening the real America outside. The statement of one member of the Anti-Saloon League was extreme but illustrative of the movement's antiurban bias: "Our nation can only be saved by turning the pure stream of country sentiment and township morals to flush out the cesspools of cities and so save civilization from pollution."[2]

```
YOU CAN'T DRINK LIQUOR AND HAVE STRONG BABIES
CAN YOU IMAGINE A COCKTAIL PARTY IN HEAVEN?
SOW ALCOHOL IN THE BODY, REAP   D isease
                                  isgrace
                                  efeat
                                  eath
FOR  My  own        Sake  I WILL BE
         brother's             A TOTAL ABSTAINER
         country's

HOW IS ALCOHOL RELATED TO   F oul     WORKS OF
                              ilthy     THE FLESH?
                              iendish

INDULGENCE IN ALCOHOL LEADS TO
                            Folly
                              Meanness
                                Sin
                                  Disgrace
                                    Misery
                                      Disease
                                        Insanity.
```

Although outnumbered in urban and industrial America, there were stalwart drys even in the area William Jennings Bryan had called "the enemy's country." New scientific data on the physiological and psychological effects of alcohol turned doctors and pharmacists toward Prohibition. (Both professions also wanted to crack down on patent medicines, which frequently contained considerable alcohol.) Even though many clergymen and urban social workers understood that drinking resulted from, as well as caused, poverty, they argued plausibly that elimination of intoxicants would help the urban poor attain a better standard of living. Some urban manufacturers supported Prohibition as a means of enhancing efficiency and industrial safety. This concern for safety also influenced the railroad brotherhoods, although other unions, including the American Federation of Labor, were at least skeptical and usually hostile. And an occasional city voted itself dry under "local option" legislation enacted in several states.

By the outbreak of the First World War, two-thirds of the states were dry, so the three-fourths majority necessary to cap the move-

Defective Children Increased With ALCOHOLIZATION of FATHERS

Among the Defects were Epilepsy, Feeble-mindedness and St. Vitus Dance

219 Children of Occasional Drinkers
2.3% DEFECTIVE

130 Children of Regular Moderate Drinkers
4.6% DEFECTIVE

67 Children of Regular Heavy Drinkers
9% DEFECTIVE

53 Children of Drunkards
19% DEFECTIVE

Alcoholism and Defects of Brain and Nerves Go Hand in Hand

ment with a constitutional amendment seemed well within reach. The war arrived most opportunely for the Anti-Saloon League, which skillfully appealed to the spirit of self-sacrifice, the willingness to conserve foodstuffs and grain, the need for industrial and military efficiency. In a time of suspicion of all things German, brewers, saloonkeepers, and many beer drinkers were manifestly German. In passing the Volstead Act and proposing the Eighteenth Amendment, Congress accurately represented a great many constituents.

But in their (nonalcoholic) celebration, drys discounted too quickly the entrepreneurial opportunity Prohibition created and the

53

political importance of areas that until the Volstead Act had remained defiantly wet. The scattered population of smaller states had outvoted the concentrated population of states like New York, Illinois, Pennsylvania, and Missouri, where the cities, factories, and saloons were located. Drys believed they had won a moral victory as well as a legislative one; they thought they had convinced their opponents as well as outflanked them politically. The drys were pragmatic lobbyists, but they overestimated the force of law, in part, at least, because they were themselves law abiding. But many other citizens did not share the drys' sober habits, good will, moral assumptions, and reverence for law. After the enactment of Prohibition, that number grew—and social conflict as well.

"THE WICKEDEST CITY IN THE WORLD"

In Chicago, the dry millennium opened with the theft of $100,000 worth of medicinal whiskey less than an hour after the Volstead Act took effect. Elsewhere in the city that night an armed band stole several barrels of alcohol from a bonded government warehouse, and hijackers diverted a truck full of illegal whiskey from a venturesome bootlegger who tried to stock his shelves too early. These were the nation's first post-Prohibition thefts of alcohol. Before the fourteen-year dry "experiment" ended, Chicago stood first on other rosters: federal agents raided their first speakeasy in Chicago; one of the city's newspapers charged that the underworld in Chicago had a "closer and sweeter" relationship with municipal politicians than existed in "any other American city"; the Illinois convocation of Congregational clergy nominated Chicago as "The Wickedest City in the World."[3]

What looked to a preacher like sin seemed a wonderful opportunity to Johnny Torrio. In three attempts between 1919 and 1926, Chicago's drys had never mustered the support of 200,000 voters; the total wet vote never fell below 400,000. Torrio liked that kind of market, and he urged his boss, James ("Big Jim") Colosimo, to add liquor to the services he already supplied in his brothels and restaurants. In addition to an existing system of distribution, Torrio

"Big Jim" Colosimo

argued, Colosimo's competitive advantages included political connections that minimized any risk. Policemen all over the city owed
"Big Jim" money, and judges and politicians owed him favors in
return for votes he had delivered in the past and might withhold in
the future. But Colosimo, Chicago's first Italian vice magnate—
prosperous, contented, perhaps bemused by his new wife—decided
not to enlarge the business. An unknown gunman, probably
imported from New York, whence Torrio himself had come a
decade earlier, killed Colosimo in May 1920, before rivals began to
provide for all those potential customers.

Many businessmen in the 1920s denounced competition as wasteful, a doctrine to which Johnny Torrio subscribed. After Colosimo's

55

murder, Torrio established a trade association—a criminal cartel—designed to end the competitive chaos in Chicago's liquor supply. Although he could not adopt every innovative managerial technique developed during the decade, Torrio used old ones that seemed applicable. He divided the territory among various claimants, saw to the corruption of law-enforcement officials, guarded supplies from the raids of competitors, and made connections with importers and distillers in other areas. He bought breweries and went into production as well as distribution. He and his associates fixed the price of beer and then raised it after they had perfected their monopoly. He retained Colosimo's gambling and vice operations, thereby diversifying his holdings. When restless members of the firm encroached on the territory of other partners, or when outsiders tried to interfere, Torrio reacted ruthlessly.

Al Capone, Torrio's vice president in charge of ruthlessness, explicitly represented himself as a businessman. "Some call it boot-

Johnny Torrio

Al Capone

legging," Capone admitted; "I call it a business." It was such a thriving business, indeed, that he needed no "high pressure salesmen." He simply supplied a receptive market with good products at a fair price:

> If people didn't want beer and wouldn't drink it, a fellow would be crazy for going around trying to sell it. I've seen gambling houses, too ... and I never saw anyone point a gun at a man and make him go in. I've never heard of anyone being forced to go to a place to have some fun. . . . [M]y booze has been good and my games have been on the square. . . . I've always regarded it as a public benefaction if people were given decent liquor and square games.[4]

Capone's apology had several significant omissions, including intimidation, extortion, and murder. He was no ordinary business-man, nor even an ordinary crook anxious to wrap himself in the prestige Americans in the 1920s accorded their business leaders. Capone had no need of borrowed prestige; he was one of the charismatic people of the time, with a public recognition comparable to that of Babe Ruth, Henry Ford, or Charles A. Lindbergh. Sightseeing buses took the route past Capone's office. Crowds buzzed when he went to the races. To the press, he was "The Big Fellow," one of the wonders of Chicago, the most famous of the nation's gangsters, an authentic folk hero.

But it was not his businessman's posture so much as what he said that engaged the attention of responsible journalists and fascinated the public. Capone confirmed in colorful (and probably laundered) language the universal suspicion that hypocrisy cloaked a nation of self-righteous lawbreakers. Sometimes he pointed directly to the white-collar parallels to blue-collar crime. "When I sell liquor it's bootlegging," Capone remarked; "when my patrons serve it on silver trays . . . it's hospitality."[5] Gambling was illegal, but betting on the stock market in the 1920s was investing. Rigging a roulette wheel was immoral, but fixing the price of steel was good business. Bribery was corrupting, but buying out a competitor at an inflated price was shrewd management. "The Big Fellow" had no original sociological insight. But his observations on lawbreaking deserved the public hearing they received; on that subject, he was an expert.

The long history of the nation's fascination with its outlaws derives in part from a guilty suspicion that the underworld is, as Capone implied, the straight society stripped of moral pretense. The narrow line between criminal and respectable conduct has appealed to novelists and filmmakers, who have sometimes depicted the underworld as a new frontier, where the simple virtues of strength, courage, loyalty, and intelligence are still rewarded. In this view, crime may become the social escalator out-groups once found in education and business, the competitive shortcut for those whose talents a bureaucratized society ignores. "I tried," Al Capone once complained, "to get into legitimate business two or three times."

Although this model has no inherent ethnic limitations, it has been applied most frequently to Italians; the Italian-American gangster was a stereotype when the twentieth century began. Irish police in Lawrence had needed no prodding to arrest Italian agitators because everyone knew that Italians were violent and broke the law. The United States Immigration Commission certified the criminal aptitude of the entire national group: "certain kinds of criminality are inherent in the Italian race." In this view, crime was imported, not bred in the slums of Lawrence or Chicago.[6]

Sociologists at the University of Chicago had another hypothesis. Like progressives before the war, and like most reformers of any era, these investigators assumed that environment explained unacceptable conduct better than heredity. The notion that "old-world traits" accounted for crime, John Landesco wrote in his study of *Organized Crime in Chicago* (1929), was "the purest banality." Instead, he concluded, the gangster "is a product of his surroundings in the same way in which a good citizen is a product of his environment."[7]

A judge from New York agreed. "Despite the popular impression to the contrary," the judge told a Senate committee in 1926, the criminals in his courtroom were not foreign-born. Rather they were sons of immigrants, "brought up under the aegis of our free institutions and under the American system of education and training." Indeed, the judge seemed to be saying that American education and institutions—presumably the same instruction and institutions that produced upright citizens—produced criminals. His syntax was badly tangled and the judge may not have meant to go that far. But others meant precisely what he had said—the successful entrepreneur and the ambitious criminal might well come from the same American mold. They could have learned the same lessons as children, perhaps in the same neighborhoods, the same churches, the same schools.[8]

This network of shared urban experience often left out would-be reformers, even when they were themselves urban residents. Reformers did not gamble, or frequent saloons and whorehouses, or bribe public officials and policemen. Reformers did not even know people who practiced that sort of vice, or the municipal authorities

This Ben Shahn painting, showing the futility of Prohibition, traces a shipment from the rumrunner in the background to the drunk in the street. A smiling Al Capone looks at customers and a Temperance poster.

who were supposed to suppress it. Indeed these reformers, one historian has concluded, "approached criminal justice with values and life experiences that differed from those of city politicians." Those who tried to disrupt the early twentieth-century network of crime and corruption in Chicago were "outsiders"—made so by residence, wealth, attitude, and values. Chicago's "criminals" and the city's "authorities" maintained a relationship based in part, as "reformers" suspected, on bribery and political favors. But the relationship also grew from the common experience of growing up in a city, from a sympathetic understanding of the needs of other groups, from mutual accommodation, from a morality less dogmatic than that of reformers. Both "criminals" and "authorities" were of the city, not outside it.[9]

In particular, many urban officials found a saloon more tolerable than did rural Americans. That acceptance derived in part from the fact that small-town saloons were often as disreputable as the Anti-Saloon League charged, while those in cities could be almost respectable. The Committee of Fifty, a group of temperance advocates less extreme than the ASL, understood that a saloon might serve as a democratic men's club and meet a legitimate social need. "The doors swing open before any man who chooses to enter," the committee noted: the customer was "taken as he is, and . . . given what he wants." The committee realized that many saloons were not benign but suggested that society admit their social functions, which other institutions must provide if saloons were to be abolished. "When a man sees outside of the saloon what is more attractive than what he finds in it, he will cease to be its patron," the committee concluded.[10]

The most attractive saloon in the nation, attended by the most attentive of the nation's saloonkeepers, was located on Chicago's Archey Road, which stretched "from the heart of an ugly city to the cabbage gardens." There, "not far from the polis station," Mr. Dooley dispensed Irish wit and presumably an occasional glass of Irish whiskey to Mr. Hennessey and to Finley Peter Dunne, the eavesdropping journalist who invented Mr. Dooley for the *Chicago Post* in the 1890s. With detached amusement, Mr. Dooley watched

Speakeasies and gangster hangouts
in Chicago and Cicero

the waves of reform dash against the rocks of social institutions and human fallibility. It was a great mistake, Mr. Dooley had noticed, "to think that annywan ra-aly wants to rayform." In fact, he continued: "You nivir heard iv a man rayformin' himsilf. He'll rayform other people gladly."[11] When reformers preached against drink, Mr. Dooley's eloquence was roused: "Ivry statesman in this broad land is in danger iv gettin' wather-logged because whiniver he sees a possible vote in sight he yells f'r a pitcher iv ice wather an' dumps into himself a basin iv that noble flooid that in th' more rugged days iv th' republic was on'y used to put out fires an' sprinkle th' lawn."[12] Whiskey, on the other hand, was worth drinking:

> No, whisky ain't food. I think better iv it thin that. . . . Father Kelly puts it r-right. . . . "Hot whisky is good f'r a cold heart, an' no whisky's good f'r a hot head," he says. "Th' minyit a man relies on it f'r a crutch he loses th' use iv his legs. 'Tis a bad thing to stand on, a good thing to sleep on, a good thing to talk on, a bad thing to think on. If it's in th' head in th' mornin' it ought not to be in th' mouth at night. If it laughs in ye, dhrink; if it weeps, swear off. It makes some men talk like good women, an' some women talk like bad men. It is a livin' f'r orators an' th' death iv bookkeepers. It doesn't sustain life, but whin taken hot with wather, a lump iv sugar, a piece iv lemon peel, an' just th' dustin' iv a nutmeg-grater, it makes life sustainable."

Obviously moved, Hennessey asked if Dooley himself thought that whiskey sustained life. "It has sustained mine f'r many years," answered the genial saloonkeeper.[13]

As Mr. Dooley's establishment was the urban saloon at its best, so his wry good humor was urban sophistication at its best. The saloon could not be frequented, nor Dunne's wit enjoyed, by those who found intolerable the ambiguity of Father Kelly's views on whiskey. Crusaders are rarely wry, and their morality rarely permits ambiguity. Drinking by anyone in any place seemed to conscientious drys a threat to the entire moral order. The businessman who broke the law by drinking in his back office, Wayne Wheeler warned, "cannot consistently blame his clerks in the front office who forge checks or steal." Morality for Wheeler was indivisible: "It is either loyalty to the country or to the outlawed traffic; playing the game fair or foul."[14]

In Chicago, the game was played both fair and foul: there were rules, but they were not those of the Eighteenth Amendment and the Volstead Act. The result was not quite the best of all possible worlds, but it satisfied the needs of several social groups. Drys wrote the laws, wets drank anyhow, and gangsters collected the profits without blowing a single safe—almost like the businessmen they said they were.

DEATH AND TAXES

Johnny Torrio's business prospered. Indeed, Chicago's bootleggers made profits sufficient to corrupt about 60 percent of the police force, according to the estimate of the chief in 1923. An official of the Prohibition Bureau, looking into enforcement for President Herbert Hoover's national commission, reported that trial of a "felony liquor case by a criminal court" had become "practically a lost art." John Landesco's survey of Chicago crime noted that "only the underlings receive punishment," which was almost always trivial.[15] Of course, had the police apprehended even a small fraction of the city's alky-cookers and bootleggers, and had the city prosecuted them, the courts would have been jammed for a year dealing with a month's arrests.

No city had resources adequate to cope with crime on that scale, and Chicago's were more inadequate than most. The police force had thirteen chiefs in twenty-five years, and that kind of discontinuity would have produced disorganization and inefficiency even if every cop had been honest. While "Commissioners of police come and go, mayors succeed mayors, [and] state's attorneys are supplanted by their successors," Landesco remarked, "the leaders and followers in the ranks of organized crime remain the same." The city should take a lesson from the efficient continuity of successful outlaws.[16]

To maintain that continuity, Torrio prudently decided to move out of Chicago, for he expected the election of 1923 to upset his

"Big Bill" Thompson throws out the first ball, 1927.

understanding with the municipal government. A wave of reform threatened to end the implausible political career of William Hale ("Big Bill") Thompson, who had been Chicago's mayor since 1915. Born to prosperous parents, Thompson had been a cowboy and football player before he won a seat on the Board of Aldermen as the champion of playgrounds for the city's children, of whom he was probably the oldest and largest. As mayor, Thompson catered to the city's ethnic voting blocs, including the blacks, whom he had failed completely in the bloody race riot of 1919, though wags continued to call City Hall "Uncle Thomp's cabin." By 1923, Thompson's closest associates stood in court accused of stealing more than $1 million in school funds. The mayor tested the political climate and withdrew, leaving his office to William E. Dever, an honest judge and a hopeful reformer.

By that time, Torrio and Capone had chosen Cicero, a western suburb inhabited largely by factory workers of Bohemian descent. The saloons in Cicero defied Prohibition, but there was no organized prostitution and only a few slot machines when Torrio moved in. Cicero's racketeers were small-timers, lacking the imagination to see what the automobile and a reform administration in Chicago might do for business.

Without consulting those racketeers or their kept politicians, Torrio leased a house in Cicero and installed twenty whores. Municipal police promptly arrested the women and closed the house. Two days later, deputies of Cook County's sheriff swept into Cicero and confiscated the slot machines that had supplemented the income of the saloonkeepers and politicians of the suburb. These small-time hoodlums correctly guessed that a nudge from Torrio had inspired the sheriff's sudden zeal. The raid carried Torrio's message: if he could not establish whorehouses, they could not control gambling. Negotiation produced compromise. Torrio did not disturb existing local arrangements, but he did open gambling houses and sell beer in new locations in the city; he agreed, for the moment, not to import more whores. Within a year Cicero had more than 150 speakeasies, dozens of gambling establishments, one of which reputedly had the

Al Capone's headquarters in Cicero

largest roulette stakes in the Midwest, and slot machines handy in tobacco and candy stores. Neither the local constabulary nor the sheriff of Cook County seemed to notice.[17]

Local politicians, like local gangsters, invited Torrio's cooperation. Worried that reform might spread from Chicago, Cicero's ruling Republicans asked Capone, acting for the vacationing Torrio, to insure their success in the municipal election of 1924. Subtlety was not Capone's style: he imported about two hundred thugs to see that the right candidates won. Their weapons in full view, Capone's troops patrolled the polls asking voters how they planned to vote, marking their ballots for them, and forcing stubborn Democrats out of line.

Victorious Republicans may have expected to control Capone, but the shoe was on the other foot. When the mayor was too slow to follow instructions, the "Big Fellow" went to city hall, pushed "His Honor" down the steps, and kicked him when he tried to regain his feet and dignity. An unconcerned Cicero policeman watched. When the city council began to debate a resolution Capone had already disapproved, his messenger disrupted the meeting and thrashed some of the councilmen. Sensitive about Cicero's growing reputation for sin and violence, the mayor asked defensively what made Cicero different from Chicago, for instance. The anonymous quip in response—"when you smell gunpowder, you're in Cicero"—hardly served the mayor's purpose.[18]

About the time Torrio and Capone decided to call Cicero home, Robert St. John began to edit a new weekly newspaper there. He and his partner believed their *Cicero Tribune* could run more important stories than the social notes that filled the existing paper. St. John investigated fraudulent bids and kickbacks to politicians by those who paved Cicero's streets. He spent a night talking with a woman in one of the syndicate's brothels and splashed that story all over the *Tribune.* Aroused citizens protested without result to Cicero's police and then engaged an arsonist, who waited until the house was deserted in mid-morning and touched off a spectacular fire. Word reached St. John that Capone thought investigative journalism in Cicero had gone far enough.

Even after Ralph Capone and some friends administered an instructional beating in the middle of a Cicero street, St. John wanted to press on. The editor then had a rather pleasant conversation with the "Big Fellow," who paid St. John's hospital bills and offered to compensate him for other medical expenses, inconvenience, and wages lost as a result of the exuberance of the gangster's brother and his employees. They were, Capone explained, annoyed with St. John and drunk; the incident would not recur. Capone indicated that future cooperation might be more profitable than the animosity of the past; he offered to advertise in the *Tribune.* St. John spurned Capone's money and lost his paper. The "Big Fellow" bought out St. John's partner, and the editor moved on.[19]

The judicious use of money was more Torrio's style than Capone's. If Capone was the "Big Fellow"—self-dramatizing and profane—Torrio wanted to be an unobserved little fellow—self-effacing and tasteful. Torrio did not shrink from violence, but he preferred to use cash instead. For some of his partners, a reporter from the *Chicago Tribune* observed, crime was a "wild adventure; for Torrio, it was a business."[20]

Those ambitious adventurers kept interfering with Torrio's cartel. His inclination was to negotiate, to reallocate territories and profits, to invite powerful outsiders in, to avoid internal dissent and corporate bickering. But some junior partner always chafed under Torrio's arrangements. This intramural rivalry often seemed to end in the death of someone, too often of several people. Murder led to more murder, a form of competition Torrio thought particularly wasteful. For a while, he held the slaughter within limits he regarded as tolerable: fewer than forty in 1922 and fewer than sixty in 1923. But in 1924, Dion O'Banion served notice that he would no longer obey all of Torrio's rules. Other partners complained of O'Banion's encroachment. He began to cultivate political connections independent of Torrio and then arranged Torrio's arrest in May 1924. Six months later, O'Banion died, six bullets in his body. The grapevine, which reached the coroner's office, had it that two of Torrio's associates, bootleggers whose territory O'Banion had invaded, and two professional triggermen had killed O'Banion. The assassination

Anna O'Banion, pictured with her husband, whom she described as an ordinary homebody, "never late to dinner, always loving to fool with the radio."

could not have occurred without the consent, and perhaps the assistance, of Capone and Torrio.[21]

Torrio left Chicago for a nervous vacation. Capone, characteristically, had something to say. O'Banion had been "getting along," Capone remarked condescendingly, "better than he had any right to expect."

> But, like everyone else, his head got away from his hat. . . . Johnny Torrio had taught O'Banion all he knew and then O'Banion grabbed some of the best guys we had and decided to be boss of the booze racket in Chicago. . . . When he broke away, for a while it wasn't so good. He knew the ropes and got running us ragged. It was his funeral.[22]

And what a funeral it was! The archdiocese of Chicago denied the family a requiem mass and burial in consecrated ground, but otherwise O'Banion went first class to his reward. As the breathless papers reported, the body "lay in state" for three days on a marble slab graced head and foot with silver angels and golden candlesticks.

Dion O'Banion is shot
in his flower shop

The mile-long cortege to the cemetery stopped traffic for twenty minutes in the Loop, the city's busiest area. While Chicago's mounted police managed the crowds, a suburban force furnished the honor guard.

Public interest in O'Banion's funeral and in the grotesque, sentimental reporting of it both stirred and satisfied curiosity about gangsters. The press paid more attention to O'Banion than to Henry Cabot Lodge, who died at the same time. Several clergymen lamented the low public morality that permitted adulation of criminals. A reporter for the *Chicago Tribune,* disgusted with the coverage in his own paper, wrote that O'Banion's funeral epitomized "a great city's crawling acceptance of lawlessness" and its "glorification of worthless, dangerous men."[23]

John Landesco thought there was more to be said. For his study of organized crime, he collected data on a decade of funerals of Chicago's gangland elite. Pomp and ostentation, he concluded, were

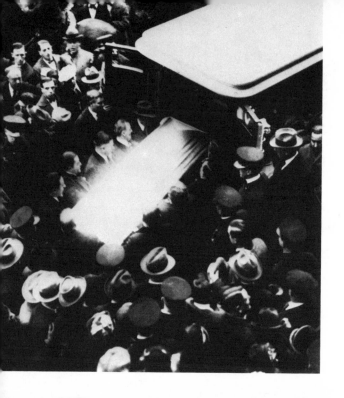

Floral effigies, fancy caskets, and crowds: funerals for Chicago's gangsters

significant, if superficial, indexes of success. The peculiar combination of mourners—civil leaders and politicians, gangsters and their outriders, police and humble working people—suggested to Landesco the complex network of friendships that developed in the city's ethnic neighborhoods. "In the hour of death," he wrote, "personal ties are disclosed which in life were concealed." These human relationships mingled crime and politics, and often small business as well, in a web that spread over much of the city. Urban politics, Landesco knew, rested upon personal loyalties and friendship, which counted for more than parties and laws. Repeated attempts to "reform" government had failed to take account of that fact and had also failed to recognize that a government based on friendship might seem to many people more effective than one that was sternly impartial.

> Residents of the so-called bluestocking wards frequently receive the erroneous impression that if the ballots in the river [i.e. "boss-ridden"] wards were freely cast and honestly counted they would show a majority against the boss, his henchmen, and his gangster allies. Nothing could be farther from the truth. . . . What needs to be appreciated is the . . . genuine popularity of the gangster, home-grown in the neighborhood gang, idealized in the morality of the neighborhood.[24]

As the 1920s wore on and funerals of gangsters proliferated, Landesco noted a significant change. Ostentation and attendance declined; the ceremonies gradually revealed less about the city's social network or the neighborhoods of a dead man's youth. The shift, Landesco thought, might reflect the stern disapproval of newspapers and churches. But more important was "the profound change that is taking place in the nature of the relations of organized crime and machine politics." Many of the new leaders of Chicago's underworld were outsiders who had not matured on Chicago's South Side. Cash, Landesco concluded, rather than friendship, had become the cement that bound criminals to one another—and to the politicians who were supposed to police them.[25]

The phenomenon was not restricted to criminals and not limited to Chicago. In a time of fabled (if in some respects illusory) prosperity and easy money, cash frequently served instead of friendship;

business relationships replaced personal relationships, and contract and receipt replaced handshake and wink. Assimilation, migration to the suburbs, and personal mobility scattered urban neighborhoods. The acquaintances of adults often were not the playmates of the schoolyard. Worldliness and sophistication replaced as ideals the secure parochialism that fostered friendship in small towns and urban neighborhoods. Chain stores moved in on "ma-'n-pa" groceries; network radio, Hollywood movies, and national magazines challenged the authority of those who determined local fashions and manners; automobiles facilitated escape from communities that seemed too confining. The nation's attention expanded in the 1920s beyond the front porch and Main Street, even if those landmarks were still the boundaries of actual experience. Regional differences remained in practice, but new trends in management, politics, fashion, leisure, and luxury spread across the land, intriguing and sometimes converting the population.

In a sense, then, the emergence in the Chicago underworld of Johnny Torrio and Al Capone was symptomatic of other changes in American society. Neither had been born or raised in Chicago; neither was part of the network of childhood relationships that the funeral of O'Banion revealed. Using techniques developed to control legitimate large-scale business, Torrio increased profits and diminished the entrepreneurial freedom of criminals of limited, local vision. Late in the decade, both Torrio and Capone joined negotiations that had as their object the formation of a national cartel. For three days, gangsters of all ethnic backgrounds, with connections throughout the country, met in Atlantic City, where all the nation's tycoons convened. "I told them," Capone said later, that "there was business enough to make us all rich and it was time to stop all the killings and look on our business as other men look on theirs. . . . [W]e finally decided to forget the past . . . and we drew up a written agreement and each man signed on the dotted line."[26]

By the middle of the decade, a federal official guessed that gross profits from Capone's varied enterprises approached $70 million annually. Bribes, fines, political contributions, and other business expenses cut into the syndicate's net income. But taxes did not, an

75

"Summer shack of a struggling young bootlegger"

oversight Capone would have cause to regret. A businessman to the end, Capone fell victim to the zealous accountants in the Internal Revenue Service. Whatever his other offenses, Capone went to jail for Tax evasion—a white-collar crime.

THE "WAVE OF UPLIFT" EBBS

If bootlegging had simply been one of the growth industries of the 1920s, Americans might have debated Prohibition with less passion and worried less about the corrupt interaction of business and government. But to its supporters Prohibition seemed the last ditch protecting the republic, the family, religion, and thrift from the assault of a new ethic. Those who defended traditional morality feared that any compromise would abandon a fundamental principle, that one broken thread would endanger the entire fabric of American life. Any little doubt became a summons to Armageddon, any flapper an affront to all decent women, any stein of beer an intolerable burden for the nation's troubled soul. The "jazz age," then, and all those fascinating symbols of it that had lured Robert St. John back to Chicago, betokened the nation's decadence rather than cosmopolitan maturity.

The influential journalist Walter Lippmann called the struggle to repeal the Eighteenth Amendment "a test of strength between social orders." The end of Prohibition, Lippmann predicted, would signify "the fall . . . of the older civilization" and the "emergence of the cities as the dominant force in America."[27] Lippmann overstated the case, for cultural conflict between village and city had not begun with Prohibition, would not end with repeal nor have a decisive victor. Rather, the traditional ethic, associated with the village, survived amid skyscrapers in a curious cultural amalgam that reflected both the nation's rural past and its modern urban sophistication: the village persisted in cities and the city overran the villages. So residents of Chicago were paradoxically proud and ashamed of the city's reputation for wickedness. They denounced the city's "social evil" without seriously disrupting traffic at whorehouses that stayed open for decades. They elected a reform mayor in 1923 and turned him out four years later for "Big Bill" Thompson, who boasted that he was "wetter than the middle of the Atlantic Ocean." They condemned and then explained away crime as an unfortunate byproduct of other virtues: the "prevalence of crime in Chicago and in America," Andrew Bruce claimed in his introduction to *Organized Crime in Chicago*, was *"due to our very newness and our very democracy."*[28] Bruce implied that nothing was really wrong, that years would work the same beneficent effect on the city that they would have on the raw whiskey criminals sold, that cities would outgrow crime and rediscover village virtue.

Meanwhile, however, crime seemed to pay, a condition that seemed likely to endure as long as the Volstead Act remained on the 77 books and the Eighteenth Amendment in the Constitution. Walter Lippmann pointed to a constitutional crisis: the drys had enough political strength to block repeal, but not enough to make wets obey the law. Lippmann could see no good way out. Perhaps, he wrote, a federal court might subvert the clear intent of Congress through a tortured interpretation of the Volstead Act. Failing that, pragmatic nullification, like the fate of the Fourteenth and Fifteenth Amendments, was the best suggestion Lippmann had.[29]

Nullification was not available to Mayor William Dever, who genuinely wanted to give Chicago honest government. At the beginning of his term, his determination had led to rhetorical excess when he claimed the city's liquor business was "dead beyond recall." Under Dever's prodding, both federal and local authorities had created a great show of law enforcement that produced much publicity and a few guilty pleas from a few little bootleggers. Then in 1924 O'Banion's murder and funeral revealed to the mayor, perhaps for the first time, the dimensions of the problem. When he asked for public support, nothing happened. His own administration, for all his good intent, was demonstrably entangled with criminals.

In the spring of 1926, saddened, perplexed, and exhausted, Mayor Dever talked about Prohibition with a committee of the United States Senate. The nation's mayors, Dever said, had responsibilities for the health, education, welfare, and security of urban residents. Yet day after day, problems related to Prohibition distracted him from those matters. He found it "almost impossible to give anything approaching good government," by which Dever seemed to mean not only honest administration but also intelligent consideration of new policies. And he had had it; "I want to be relieved. . . ."

The mayor did not mean he would resign; indeed he ran for reelection and lost badly in 1927. Rather Dever meant that he wanted Prohibition to go away. He wanted elections that did not turn on a candidate's stand on the Volstead Act. He wanted to be able to count on the loyalty of bureaucrats and the moral support of citizens. He wanted to provide better municipal services instead of more gunplay.

"The Hydra-Headed Monster"

Dever had no use for the moral arrogance of either side. There were, he thought, sincere people and high principles in both groups. The temperance people

> have honest opinions and are interested in saving the human race. They are interested in building up American citizenship. They are interested in that almost divine purpose of driving drunkenness out of human existence.

On the other hand, in "Chicago particularly, and other great cities," a "great majority" believed that

> these prohibition laws are seriously interfering with ... personal human rights ... that they have received from their ancestors as part of a social compact; that it was never agreed in that compact that anybody would have the right to control them in the matter of what they desire to eat or drink.

79

Mayor William Dever

Even if the government miraculously stamped out bootlegging, Mayor Dever said, people would brew their own alcohol at home, protected by the search and seizure provisions of the Constitution. The price of the enforcement drys demanded, he implied, was overbearing government. The mayor had a good word for village morality and another for urban sophistication, but none for too much government.[30]

Partly because of Prohibition, other efforts to achieve reform through legislation in the 1920s encountered a reawakened popular suspicion of too much government. The progressive journal *The Outlook* noted a growing disenchantment with "the great wave of uplift" that spread well beyond Prohibition.[31] For many national politicians, including those who occupied the White House, governmental inaction was neither a new nor an uncongenial idea; progressive reform had never appealed to Warren G. Harding or Calvin Coolidge. But Mayor Dever, whose convictions were progressive, had hoped to use political power to improve conditions in Chicago so that the city's residents might improve their lives. Time and again, Prohibition had stymied his effort, and in 1926 he had run out of inspiration. He would advise humility, patience, and tolerance, he told the attentive senators; after that, he did not know what to do.

Notes

[1] Robert St. John, *This Was My World* (Garden City, N.Y.: Doubleday, 1953), pp. 13, 107, 108, 109.

[2] James H. Timberlake, *Prohibition and the Progressive Movement* (Cambridge: Harvard University Press, 1963), p. 151.

[3] The fourth volume of the report issued by the Wickersham Commission, which investigated enforcement of Prohibition, discusses in detail the situation in Chicago: U.S., Congress, Senate, *Official Records of the National Commission on Law Observance and Enforcement*, 71st Cong., 3d sess., Senate Document 307, vol. IV, p. 394. See also *Literary Digest*, January 17, 1925, p.12.

[4] *Wickersham Report*, vol. IV, p. 415; see also Kenneth Allsop, *The Bootleggers*, revised edition (New Rochelle, N.Y.: Arlington House, 1968), pp. 349–51, and John Kobler, *Capone* (New York: Putnam, 1971), pp. 306, 209–10.

[5] Allsop, *Bootleggers*, 349; *Wickersham Report*, vol. IV, p. 415.

[6] Humbert S. Nelli, *The Italians in Chicago, 1880–1930* (New York: Oxford University Press, 1970), p. 126; see also Nelli, *The Business of Crime* (New York: Oxford University Press, 1976).

[7] John Landesco, *Organized Crime in Chicago* (Chicago: University of Chicago Press, 1968), pp. 119, 221.

[8] U.S., Congress, Senate, Committee on the Judiciary, *Hearings*, 69th Cong., 1st sess., 1926, vol. I, p. 152.

[9] Mark H. Haller, "Urban Crime and Criminal Justice: The Chicago Case," in *Journal of American History* (December 1970), p. 619ff.

[10] Quoted in Andrew Sinclair, *Prohibition: The Age of Excess* (Boston: Little Brown, 1962), p. 73.

[11] Finley Peter Dunne, *Mr. Dooley on Ivrything and Ivrybody* (New York: Dover Publications, 1963), pp. 190–91.

[12] Quoted in Sinclair, *Prohibition*, p. 152.

[13] Dunne, *Mr. Dooley*, p. 134.

[14] *Current History*, August 1925, p. 694.

[15] *Wickersham Report*, vol. IV, p. 346; Landesco, *Crime*, p. 249.

[16] Landesco, *Crime*, p. 278.

[17] *Wickersham Report,* vol. IV, p. 379.

[18] Kobler, *Capone,* chapter 8; Allsop, *Bootleggers,* pp. 58–64.

[19] St. John, *This Was My World,* chapter 5.

[20] Quoted in *Wickersham Report,* vol. IV, p. 375.

[21] *Ibid.,* vol. IV, pp. 355–66.

[22] Kobler, *Capone,* p. 132; Allsop, *Bootleggers,* pp. 83–84.

[23] Quoted in *Wickersham Report,* vol. IV, p. 366.

[24] Landesco, *Crime,* 169; see also chapter 9.

[25] *Ibid.,* p. 205.

[26] Kobler, *Capone,* p. 258.

[27] Lippmann, *Men of Destiny,* pp. 28–31, as quoted in Sinclair, *Prohibition,* p. 5.

[28] The italics are Bruce's; Landesco, *Crime,* p. 2.

[29] Walter Lippmann, "Our Predicament Under the Eighteenth Amendment," in *Harper's Magazine,* December 1926, p. 51.

[30] Dever testified before a subcommittee of the Senate Judiciary Committee; the hearings are cited in note 8. Dever's remarks are printed in vol. II, pp. 1361ff.

[31] *The Outlook,* January 16, 1924, p. 109.

Detroit in 3
Depression and War:
The 1930s and 1940s

Albert Goetz felt the bite of the March wind and decided it was time to begin. He jumped to the back of a parked truck, caught the attention of two or three thousand chilled demonstrators, and warned them against violence. "No trouble," Goetz cautioned; "no fighting."

> I understand . . . that the Dearborn police are planning to stop us. Well, we will try to get through somehow. But remember, no trouble.

The police of Dearborn, Michigan, did indeed plan to prevent the marchers from reaching the Ford Motor Company's River Rouge plant that afternoon in 1932. Municipal authorities thought the demonstration pointless, since the press had already carried the marchers' demands, which Henry Ford would not even receive, let alone consider. To Dearborn officials, the march seemed another Communist attempt to turn economic adversity to partisan advantage and to diminish Henry Ford's reputation for dealing decently

Tear gas fails to halt the "hunger march"

with his employees. So Charles D. Slamer, the acting chief of the Dearborn police, ordered the marchers to disperse, and signalled for tear gas when they kept coming.

The marchers' good will and good order dissipated with the blowing gas. They added rocks, frozen mud, and other handy debris to the gas that the wind carried back over the policemen, who retreated in surprise toward the entrance of the River Rouge. As the demonstrators approached the gate, icy water cascaded over them from a bridge that spanned the highway. Gas grenades and perhaps gunfire added to the confusion. Satisfied that the point had been made, Goetz climbed on another truck and was telling the marchers to go home and ponder their reception just as Harry Bennett, the chief of Ford's security force, skidded into the area in his car. A brick hit Bennett in the head, and his guards and the police opened fire. More than twenty of the scattering demonstrators were hit, and four died.

Carl Brooks, once a member of Ford security and in 1932 chief of Dearborn's police, had been ill on the day of the march. But he was the picture of vigorous activity a day later, asking federal officials to

arrest Goetz and other Communists, warning that any future demonstration would be blocked "as long as there is a man left on the
Dearborn police force," and searching for the Italian Communist
with a scar on his cheek who had fired the first shots. Witnesses,
Brooks said, had seen the man crouch behind an automobile and fire
six times. The witnesses were never identified, their ability to
recognize either Italians or Communists at sight never tested, and
the gunman (whose description matched Al Capone, among others)
never found. Although Bennett was hospitalized briefly and Carl
Slamer suffered a broken nose, no one ever proved that any demon-
strator had carried firearms or endangered lives.

A grand jury blamed the riot on "a few agitators who go about the
nation taking advantage of . . . industrial depression and other mis-
fortune" but refused to indict anyone. That explanation exonerated
Dearborn police and Ford security men and suited the Ford Motor
Company. Several letters to the *Detroit News*, perhaps inspired by
the company's public relations staff, praised the enlightened labor
practices of Henry Ford—the goose, in one unfortunate metaphor,

Funeral procession honoring demonstrators killed at River Rouge

Henry Ford

who laid golden eggs in Detroit. The company denied that many of the marchers had ever worked for Ford and disclaimed any responsibility for, or obligation to explain, the bloody disaster.[1]

An explanation was not hard to find. The two years before the marchers set off that blustery afternoon in 1932 had been lean years for Ford, for his workers, for the automobile industry, and for Detroit, which had been a showplace of American industrial genius and economic enterprise. Ford's assembly line still fascinated engineers, but his product no longer commanded the lion's share of the market. And the market, which in the 1920s had seemed unlimited, had contracted sharply with the rest of the economy after the stock-market crash late in 1929. Almost 450,000 workers had produced 5,337,000 cars in 1929; three years later, fewer than 250,000, earning less than half the 1929 payroll, produced 1,332,000 cars. Automobile workers, once the aristocracy of American industrial labor, began to lose their grip on the good life, to display hostility toward employers who had formerly seemed benevolent, and to wonder whether unions offered a way to hold on.

Before 1932, unions had made little headway in Detroit, particularly in the automobile plants, where the workers were among the most prosperous of the nation's industrial employees. In May 1929, as part of financial planning for production in Europe, Ford asked the Bureau of Labor Statistics to suggest wage scales that would provide European employees a standard of living comparable to that of his workers in Detroit. To establish a statistical base, the bureau studied 100 families that met its definition of average: the husband was the sole support for his wife and two or three children, and had no income except the $7 daily wage at the Ford Motor Company; he

The Ford Motor Company, River Rouge plant

had worked at least 225 days in 1929; neither dependent relatives nor paying lodgers lived in the family's single-family house or flat. The statisticians had some difficulty completing their sample, for the average was not typical. And 1929, of course, was not 1932, when unemployed automobile workers set out toward the River Rouge. Still the bureau's work did provide an authoritative measure of what the depression cost automobile workers and a numerical explanation for the predepression absence of strong unions in Detroit.

The bureau's 1929 criteria required an annual income of about $1700, more than three times what the ordinary textile worker in Lawrence had earned in 1912. Yet the bureau's sample averaged only a day's pay in annual savings. Although stew beef was too expensive for the tables of Lawrence, Ford's workers ate more roast beef than stew and almost as much steak. Every auto worker surveyed had eaten fresh oranges during the year, and fresh produce made diets in Detroit more varied than the fare available in Lawrence. To be sure, refrigeration, more efficient national distribution of food, and changing taste accounted for some of that difference. But money accounted for more.

Money also avoided some of the crowding that had characterized housing in Lawrence. Again the bureau's average predetermined its findings, for crowding among Ford's black employees resembled the situation in Lawrence and sanitary conditions were sometimes worse. Yet Ford's ordinary white employees could afford either to rent or to own (two-thirds of the sample were renters) four- or five-room dwellings "equipped with bathroom, inside toilet, running water . . . and sewer connection." In contrast to Lawrence, where two or three people per room was not uncommon, Ford's workers had at least one room available for each member of the family.

All but 1 percent of those houses had electrical service, which cost about $20 annually, but only 5 percent had a telephone, for telephone service was less prevalent and more expensive. One family in two owned (or was purchasing) an electric washing machine, one in five a vacuum cleaner, one in ten an electric refrigerator, one in three a radio, and one in two a car—almost invariably a Ford.[2]

Street scene: Paradise Valley

John Boris did not have a car, but he had finally succumbed to his children's urging that he buy a radio. A careful, diligent Slavic immigrant, Boris had left the logging camps of northern Michigan to better himself in Detroit. He found a good job, married a good wife, and bought a good house; his increasing wages kept pace with his increasing family until he had eight children and a daily wage of eight dollars. "In dose days," Boris remembered later, "work was hard all right at Ford's, but dey treat us like mens."[3]

Pat Brooks did not do quite that well, but he preferred the factories of Detroit to sharecropping in the Buckalew Mountains of east-central Alabama. Once he had a job and a place to live in Paradise Valley, the ironic phrase for Detroit's black ghetto, Brooks summoned the other fourteen members of the family to join him. The black population of Detroit, 40,000 in 1920, tripled by 1930, and made Paradise Valley as overpopulated as Pat Brooks' flat. Even if it was crowded, one of Brooks' young stepsons recalled, "the place we lived in . . . had something we didn't have in Alabama, an inside toilet [and] . . . electric lights." On the whole, Joe Louis Barrow went on, "it was nice."[4]

It was not so nice in 1930 and 1931 and 1932, when cars did not sell and workers lost their jobs. By the middle of the decade, Brooks did not need his job, for his stepson had dropped his last name and begun to collect purses as a first-rate professional boxer. As the world's heavyweight champion, Joe Louis soon had an income in six figures and unmatched prestige among American blacks.

But John Boris needed a job, even if Pat Brooks did not. Bewildered by his dismissal, Boris mused as he left the plant:

> Fourteen year . . . I work for Henry Ford. . . . When I go out of factory that day I don' believe; I don' believe he do such ting to me. I think trouble wid man in de office who don' un'erstan'.

Boris sought out Mr. Ford to clear up the misunderstanding, but guards at the employment office restrained him. Ford had his name, Boris was told; he would be called. For nine months, he remembered bitterly, "I go no work."

John Boris had saved a few hundred dollars, which disappeared after two operations on his wife and the consequent hospital bills. The bank threatened to foreclose his mortgage. One of the boys, whose command of written English excelled his father's, wrote a letter to the Ford Motor Company explaining the family's circumstances. An investigator called shortly afterward and left a slip that Boris presented at the employment office. He was assigned, at $6 per day, to the same job he had formerly done for $8 daily, and he could work only three days per week. After sixty days, he was told, he would receive a raise of a dollar a day. On the sixty-first day, he received $7; on the sixty-third day, he was fired. Not laid off; fired. "Anything wrong wid my work for comp'ny?" he asked the employment man, who shook his head. "I haf' no money now . . . lose my home quick, what I do chil'ren, what I do doctor?" The questions tumbled out, and Boris added that he had worked for Henry Ford for fourteen years. In all that time, the employment man said, ending the conversation, Boris ought to have saved some money.

"I go out from mill," the subdued, suddenly old man's narrative continued. "I use tink . . . if something come like dis, go to Henry

Ford yoursel'." But he had tried that before, so he went to a lawyer instead. The lawyer—"who knows ting like dis more what I do"—told him "Nutting, John, ain' nutting you can do."[5]

Thousands of others reached the same discouraging conclusion. In Chicago, Al Capone, who was about to be fed by the taxpayers, repaid them in advance by financing a soup kitchen for the city's unemployed that served 120,000 meals in six weeks. Frank Murphy thought Detroit's unemployed were the responsibility of the city rather than gangsters, and he promised assistance if elected mayor. Indeed, he promised more than that—honest, efficient administration, a reduction in the city's debt, care for the sick and aged, and "the dew and sunshine of a new morning."[6]

Frank Murphy's Irish tongue often outran his accomplishment, but his heart was in the right place. Freckled, red-haired, and charming, he was a "verbal tornado" at the University of Michigan's law school. He also taught English to Detroit's immigrants and they in turn taught Murphy, who had grown up in comfortable, small-town circumstances, about poverty and slums and urban life. As a compassionate judge on Detroit's criminal court, he tested some of the precepts he had learned from the Catholic social gospel movement. He was a Democrat with nonpartisan support among Detroit's ethnic groups, Catholics, blacks, and working people. Frank Murphy was not a product of the old machine politics; he was an urban liberal, the kind of Democrat who dominated his party and the nation after 1933.

Unemployment, Mayor Murphy thought after his election in the fall of 1930, was a temporary phenomenon; autumn had never been a good time for the automobile industry. When he asked the unemployed to register, about 80,000 did so in a month, of whom more than 13,000 indicated immediate, desperate need. The city's social workers estimated that 110,000 families faced the winter without income. By January 1931, the estimate had doubled and a third of the labor force was thought to be out of work. At the time of the presidential election of 1932, Detroit's Department of Public Welfare guessed that 350,000 workers—one in two—had no regular employment. At the River Rouge, the average number of employees dropped from nearly 100,000 in 1929 to less than 30,000 in 1933. Median weekly income in a district welfare officials called "typical" fell from $33.05 in 1929 to $10.82 in 1933.

By that time, Murphy did not need statistics to know about hardship. The city's newspapers and the mail in his office revealed people struggling to retain dignity, pride, and life itself. A woman used an abandoned car to shelter her four children, but she could not find enough food for herself and died of malnutrition. Another woman complained that her neighborhood had become so impoverished that begging no longer brought results. A young man, who claimed he had "left no stone unturned" in Murphy's campaign, asked the mayor to find him a job. Not necessarily a good job; "I don't ask for no tobacco in times like this." All he asked was "the necessarys." "A man has got to eat and pay his rent and get something to wear in this weather."[7]

The young man said he needed employment to sustain the faith of his new wife as well as to secure "the necessarys." As the depression ground on, many people postponed marriage, or, if married, tried to postpone children. Both the number of marriages and the birth rate in Wayne County dropped nearly a third between 1929 and 1933, a statistic that suggests sexual tension and documents social distress as insistently as do indices of unemployment. The divorce rate declined too, for the depression forced some discordant families to stay together and others to substitute mutual support for bickering. Some families were dissolved without legal process; ashamed fathers sometimes stopped coming home after days of unsuccessful job-seeking.

For many men, the depression brought personal humiliation. An unemployed man, who grew up assuming that parental and marital authority depended upon his paycheck, sometimes could not sustain one without the other. Although a working wife might save the family economically, she also proved her husband's failure to provide. An unemployed father lost face with his children, when he did not lose their affection, and the shame was compounded if they were employed. The wages of two of John Boris's daughters kept the family together, at some psychic cost to their father: "Las' July," Boris sighed, "I was a good man. . . . I ain't man now."[8]

The struggle to remain self-reliant was the final prop of the sagging pride of many families, and the reluctant decision to seek help a disgrace that was compounded when help was not readily available. Yet unemployment in Detroit and across the land quickly climbed beyond the capacity of private agencies to create jobs and private charities to provide relief. Government, Murphy said, had a "duty to the people" to furnish relief "not as a matter of charity, and not paternally, but as a matter of right." He spent the city's *annual* welfare budget in a week and rang up a deficit of $13 million in his first year in office, when relief payments sometimes reached $2 million per month and totalled $17 million. In the spring of 1931, almost one in eight residents of Detroit depended upon the municipal dole. No city in the nation made such an unreserved commitment to its citizens so early.[9]

MAYOR MURPHY TRIES TO HELP

When the depression persisted, Detroit's taxpayers, like the city's charities, could not do all that was asked. Although local and state governments collected three of every four dollars an American paid in taxes, those governments in the 1920s also provided most of the public services. And, unlike federal revenues, which derived in large measure from the income tax, revenues of local governments resulted from levies that bore no direct relationship to ability to pay. Taxes on sales, on gasoline, and especially on property, all of which required a greater proportion of the income of ordinary people than of the rich, supported local government. A large fraction of Mayor Murphy's expenditures for relief, therefore, came from precisely the working people he was trying to help.

Although Henry Ford reproved the unemployed as lazy and condemned as corrupt the bureaucrats who dispensed relief, the city's

ordinary homeowners and landlords had more reason to complain of injustice. Ford paid his taxes in suburban Dearborn—not Detroit, where the relief recipients lived, and where thrifty but unemployed citizens struggled to protect their property from foreclosure and the tax auction, while, as they saw it, the mayor handed out relief to their improvident neighbors. Property-owners could not legitimately collect relief because they had assets; on the other hand, those assets could not be sold, even at depression prices, because there were no buyers. So the taxes (and the mortgages) often went unpaid. The Department of Public Welfare found that two-thirds of the homeowners in its "typical" district owed back taxes and that the mortgages of half were in arrears. A city official estimated that overdue taxes encumbered 250,000 of Detroit's 428,000 appraised properties.[10]

Expenses always exceeded revenues and the city's fiscal crisis seemed perpetual. The municipal accounts contained evidence to support any explanation of the deficit, for budget-making had become a charade. Mayor Murphy inherited, and retained, an annual budget of $76 million, which was balanced by the polite fiction that prosperity would return before the books had to be closed. With slight annual variations, Detroit's budgets divided roughly in thirds. Uncollected taxes meant that one-third of the city's projected revenue was never received; debt service required another third; and one-third, and sometimes less, was available to operate the city and provide, if possible, for the relief of its unemployed.

Detroit's needs outstripped not only a city's revenues but those of a state as well, which, in any case, the state legislature would not make available. So Murphy sought federal help for his unbalanced budget and his hungry constituents. To give his plea added volume, he invited other mayors to come to Detroit in June 1932. They endorsed resolutions requesting federal funds for public works and federal loans for relief and municipal debt management. The convention was ceremonial: "It is not necessary for us to deliberate at length," Murphy said. "We have but one objective—help to our people, which only the federal government can give adequately."[11]

Frank Murphy speaks at
conference of mayors

Murphy carried the mayors' resolutions to congressional leaders and to President Herbert Hoover, whose early opposition to federal action had diminished as the depression wore on. Early in the year, Hoover had assented to the charter of a federal lending agency, the Reconstruction Finance Corporation (RFC), to assist the nation's financial institutions. The President and Murphy agreed that the RFC's authority to lend could be extended to municipalities. Hoover preferred such loans to several less acceptable plans that were sprouting in Congress, and he signed the Emergency Relief and Construction Act about six weeks after Murphy's visit. Detroit promptly applied for, and received, RFC loans that provided 95 percent of the city's relief funds in 1932–1933. However ineffective the RFC was as an agency of national recovery, it sustained thousands of unemployed citizens in Detroit and postponed a financial crisis that would have added another dimension to the city's distress. Murphy received a warmer welcome and more cooperation from Herbert Hoover, who was renowned neither for warmth nor cooperation, than from governors in Lansing.

The mayor's trip to Washington had symbolic as well as financial importance, for more and more Americans expected assistance from the federal government. Regulation frequently accompanied assistance, and political power gradually shifted from cities and states toward Washington. Later, local officials would protest that the federal government had usurped their authority and wrapped them in layers of red tape. Yet federal intervention had often begun because of local requests and in response to local needs.

SITTING DOWN

Nurtured on maxims about self-reliance, most Americans at first sought a personal accommodation with industrial depression. For many, the search was desperate and the odyssey unending—from Oklahoma to California, from one barred factory gate to another, from employer to bureaucrat and back, from page to page of the classified ads. Personal, local, and regional variations blurred into one nationwide portrait of an underemployed people with ebbing confidence in themselves and their society. For all their idiosyncrasies, John Boris and his family stood for a great many other Americans.

It took some time to realize that, to understand that local events were not unique, to recognize the interdependence of the elements in the nation's mass-consumption economy. The local frame of reference, which had limited the view of most Americans, needed broadening; the habit of relying on individual and local initiative needed critical examination. John Boris, Mayor Murphy, and other Americans who felt the depression had to do the best they could while the country developed a new perspective—the perspective Franklin Roosevelt called a "new deal."

Roosevelt was no economist and his phrase summarized an eclectic political program rather than a coherent theoretical approach to depression. But, however unsystematically, the Roosevelt administration eventually tried most of the devices associated with urban liberalism, and Franklin Roosevelt certainly subscribed to the urban liberal's belief that government must respond more quickly to human needs than to demands for cheap, efficient administration. Government, in this view, must do more for citizens than furnish schools and police. The nation's economic health, for instance, was too important to entrust to free enterprise; in a depression, the government should provide jobs, or at least relief, even if that required larger expenditures and a concentration of political power that would have frightened earlier liberals.

In some way, the New Deal touched the life of every citizen in the land. A mortgage was refinanced and a farm or home saved. A new gymnasium enhanced the local high school or a mural the public library. Agencies built dams and planned communities, insured bank deposits and informed investors, hired young men to plant trees, and paid farmers not to plant cotton and wheat. Many—perhaps most—communities assumed that federal assistance to the unemployed required no permanent socioeconomic or political change; the New Deal would be over when the money ran out. The long-run effects of Social Security, aggressive labor unions, and a revitalized Democratic party did not appear immediately. The New Deal's "imprint on the states," one historian has concluded, "was often faint and indistinct," as if produced by an "overused piece of carbon paper."[12]

But in Detroit the imprint was sharp and lasting. In particular, legislation passed in the Roosevelt administration fostered the growth of labor unions, a development that profoundly altered power relationships in a city where industrialists had been accustomed to having their own way. Before the Roosevelt administration ended, the United Auto Workers (UAW) and the Congress of Industrial Organizations (CIO) and the National Labor Relations Act would become as important as Ford and Chrysler and the law of supply and demand. The New Deal made an open-shop town into a citadel of organized labor and permanently modified the power structure of the community.

The old order did not pass without a struggle. Henry Ford, in particular, had an obsession with independence from partners, financiers, employees, and governmental regulations. When most of the automobile industry reluctantly complied with the National Industrial Recovery Act in the early days of the New Deal, Ford did not. When his employees showed an interest in organization, he fired them; early in his fourteen years at River Rouge, John Boris noticed that those who approved of unions soon vanished from the shop. Ford sustained Harry Bennett's ubiquitous security force in large part to "protect" employees from the blandishments of "outside agitators."

Several outsiders did in fact help the automobile workers unite. Senator Robert F. Wagner, perhaps the prototype urban liberal from New York, argued that the federal government must augment the power of independent unions in order to make collective bargaining a colloquy among equals. He introduced the National Labor Relations Act—usually called the Wagner Act—to encourage collective bargaining and to protect the right of workers to designate "representatives of their own choosing, for the purpose of negotiating the terms and conditions of their employment." The Wagner Act outlawed discrimination against union members and in favor of company unions, and required employers to negotiate in good faith.

John L. Lewis, the president of the United Mine Workers, heard the knocking of opportunity. He had for months attempted to convince the AFL that workers in mass-production industries could be organized if only craft unions would stop jurisdictional squabbling. Lewis favored an industrial form of organization, which would unite workers by plant or industry, rather than by skill or function. A man of large frame, large vocabulary, and large ambition, Lewis never backed away from a fight. Congress enacted the Wagner Act in the summer of 1935; he convened the CIO and split the AFL in the fall.

He intended to tackle the steel industry first, but impatient auto workers adhered to another schedule. Circumstances in 1935 and 1936 favored organization: the worst of the depression seemed past,

John L. Lewis

and people in Detroit were going back to work. Mounting employment reduced the number of workers available to replace "disloyal" employees who flirted with unions. The Wagner Act promised legal protection unions had not had before. The tiny organization of auto workers, apparently doomed to continuing weakness and frustration in the AFL, withdrew, asked Lewis for assistance, and assaulted General Motors at the end of 1936.

Conflict began in Atlanta and spread to GM's major factories in Flint, Michigan. The United Auto Workers (UAW) did not establish a conventional picket line. Instead strikers stayed inside the plants, preventing production, barring strikebreakers, and by implication holding the corporation's property hostage. This tactic enabled an organized minority to shut down one plant or paralyze one segment of an assembly line, thereby halting production as effectively as masses of pickets, which the UAW lacked. An agreement to bargain, reached after six weeks of tense confrontation in the GM plants in Flint, demonstrated to exhilarated auto workers the advantages of sitting down, rather than walking out.[13]

Indeed the sit-down became almost a fad in the spring of 1937. Shortly after the agreement in Flint, sit-down strikes erupted all over Detroit—in department stores, cafeterias, hotels, print shops, packing plants, and even among laborers on a federally financed relief project. When bargaining between Chrysler and the UAW reached a stalemate over exclusive bargaining rights, a shop steward received the telephoned signal "My hand is up," and Chrysler's workers sat down.[14]

It seemed a propitious moment to strike Chrysler. The UAW had already enlisted a significant number of Chrysler employees. If the proportion was smaller than the 95 percent spokesmen claimed, it was nevertheless large and probably a majority. In addition, Chrysler had in 1936 enlarged its share of the market, and management hoped to avoid any break in production that might endanger that gain. The settlement with GM placed competitive pressure on management and stimulated Chrysler's workers to seek equality. Walter Chrysler, the industry's Horatio Alger hero, had once built automobiles himself and professed a personal link with his employees that earlier year-end bonuses and improved wage schedules confirmed. Chrysler's large Dodge plant was located in Hamtramck, an enclave of Detroit where the union had considerable influence in municipal government; city officials ordered police not to assist strikebreakers, and the city council endorsed the UAW's demands by resolution.

But the proliferation of sit-down strikes, and perhaps their success, had sapped public support. A Gallup poll indicated that two voters in three favored legislation to curb the strikes. A Michigan legislator submitted a bill authorizing prosecutors to charge sit-down strikers with a felony. Progressive national politicians denounced the strikes as preludes to fascism; Franklin Roosevelt was reported weighing legislation that would authorize federal force. The president of the AFL self-righteously announced his union's opposition to sit-down strikes because they alienated the public, a position John L. Lewis dismissed as "characteristically cowardly and contemptible."

An increasingly unpopular weapon was not the UAW's only cross: the union demanded the right to bargain for every Chrysler employee, an objective the Wagner Act made legally attainable, but which much of the public did not support. Homer Martin, the UAW's president, tried to explain the difference between a union shop, which made employment contingent on union membership and was not the UAW's goal, and exclusive representation, which meant that a union chosen by a majority of the employees bargained for all, whether or not they joined the union. The distinction was not trivial, but the UAW never gained public understanding of the difference, partly because the Chrysler Corporation's public statements continually obscured it. Even before the strike, Walter Chrysler had promised to "recognize the right of any individual employee to speak for himself." As the sit-down continued, Chrysler reiterated his willingness to discuss with the UAW wages, hours, overtime, working conditions, and any subject except exclusive representation: "Men who wish to work in our plants will not be required to hold a union card to do so." Disgruntled employees and their wives picked up the theme in letters to the editor of the *Detroit News*. A union, they maintained, intimidated, harassed, and exploited contented workers, and led the United States in paths marked by Communists. During the Flint sit-down, General Motors had tried to create a public opinion hostile to the strikers; perhaps Chrysler's public-relations department mailed some of those surprisingly similar letters. Others, however, revealed the genuine emotion behind opposition to the strike: "Good God!" expostulated an anonymous correspondent:

> Is our happiness to be completely destroyed? Are all our ideals to be trampled in the dust? Are we men without honor? . . . Must we stand aside now and see communism tear down what we have struggled to build?[15]

Frank Murphy sensed this popular mood. Elected governor of Michigan in 1936, he had had to wrestle with the GM strike in Flint almost as soon as he had finished his inaugural oath. Murphy refused to use troops to evict strikers from GM plants and thus to

To emphasize Murphy's point, reportedly at his instruction, Detroit police removed sit-down strikers from several local stores and businesses. Homer Martin denounced the use of police in labor disputes and threatened to call out 100,000 pickets to defend strikers in the Chrysler plants. By that time, Murphy had bypassed Martin, who lacked the nerve and emotional stamina for prolonged bargaining. Through Roosevelt's Secretary of Labor, Frances Perkins, Murphy reached John L. Lewis, who said he would meet Walter Chrysler "on a half hour's notice." Negotiations at that level avoided the score-settling and face-saving that might have preoccupied less experienced representatives from either camp. In a few hours, Chrysler and Lewis agreed that the corporation would not resume production and the union would evacuate the plants. Once that preliminary agreement had been fulfilled, the two men would meet again to discuss designation of an exclusive bargaining agent.

The national press reported great relief in Detroit, sudden disappearance of security guards, the cessation of food-hoarding, an end

Strikers leaving Chrysler factory after settlement was reached

to talk about general strikes and revolutions.[16] Those reports exaggerated the community's tension. Local reporters had seen no friction between police and the good-natured crowd at the union's enormous rally in Cadillac Square. The event had been "far more orderly than the celebration of the Detroit Tigers winning the World Series," noted the condescending *Free Press*, "and only about one-tenth the size."[17] According to state police, strikers left the Chrysler plants without damage, in "unusually good condition." The UAW mustered a happy band of pickets, who cheered as Lewis and Chrysler polished the final contract.

When it was signed, the union had gained little that Chrysler would not have conceded without a strike. The company recognized the UAW as the agent for its members only, thus preserving the principle Chrysler regarded as central. To help save the union's face, he promised not to subvert the UAW or to assist other unions, and not to discriminate against union members in hiring. In return, the UAW pledged no harassment of nonunion employees and no sit-down strikes while the contract was in force. Local representatives

UAW rally at Cadillac Square

of labor and management pencilled in details of wages and hours, and production started once more.[18]

Yet, whatever the UAW's contractual concessions, the union had succeeded. Workers had compelled the corporation's president to bargain with their representative. They had forced both General Motors and Chrysler to acknowledge that employees had a right to voice demands, which sometimes had to be heeded. They had trimmed corporate power and invaded property rights. They had every reason to cheer as Lewis and Chrysler finished the agreement.

But the celebrating strikers themselves did not sign that agreement, and they had not won the strike alone. They had had the organizing help of the United Mine Workers and the CIO, and the negotiating skill and experience of John L. Lewis. They had secured from Governor Murphy a neutrality that bordered on benevolence. They had had the interested intervention of the secretary of labor and, more remotely, of the President of the United States. And sustaining the actions of all of these people was the National Labor Relations Act and the rather recent principle that workers were entitled to "representatives of their own choosing."

Few of those vital allies were local. As mayor of Detroit, Frank Murphy might have been sympathetic, but it was as governor that he had effectively nullified a strike-breaking injunction. No city council could require collective bargaining as did the Congress of the United States. Local officials of the UAW, however determined and well intentioned, lacked the stature of John L. Lewis; they did not even attend many of the most important bargaining sessions. And, appropriately enough, the contract was not signed in Detroit. A labor dispute in Detroit, like massive unemployment there, was no mere local matter.

Federal economic intervention, Herbert Hoover had warned in the early days of the depression, would undermine the independence of states and cities and free individuals. So long as that intervention was limited to the distribution of federal funds, most Americans ignored, and even ridiculed, Hoover's caution. Yet the Wagner Act and some of the other legislation of the New Deal was intervention of quite a different sort. The New Deal did not create the intricate, centralized economy that made the vitality of the automobile industry, for instance, a legitimate national concern; that was the reason for federal intervention that Hoover had overlooked. But the New Deal did encourage the unions that, in the view of some Chrysler employees, endangered individual independence and livelihood. However mistaken Hoover had been about the cause, he had correctly predicted diminished local control of important aspects of American life.

THE BATTLE AT THE OVERPASS

Leaders of the UAW announced that Ford was next, but they were whistling in the dark. They knew that April was too late in the model year for an effective strike, and that they had less support and more determined opposition at the River Rouge than at Chrysler. A rumor that Henry Ford might close the plant swept Detroit and was denied. But for several weeks he left floating a story that he would outbid the UAW with a dramatic wage increase; that speculation eventually died for lack of substantiation. He claimed that the Wagner Act was unconstitutional, a tenable stance until the Supreme Court, with ironically apt timing, upheld the law a week after the Chrysler settlement. Ford then dismissed the act as irrelevant because his employees did not want to join a union anyhow. Even if they did, he added, he would not recognize it, and anyone who sat down would be carried out.[19]

At the urging of John L. Lewis, the union decided to enroll Ford's workers through an old-fashioned organizing drive. Richard Frankensteen and Walter Reuther, two ambitious, young UAW officials took charge of the campaign. They leased offices in Dearborn, secured a permit to pass out leaflets, and picked about sixty volunteers for the first distribution. Since Reuther and Frankensteen wanted to demonstrate the union's pacific intent, many of those selected were women. To insure their safety, and to make possible an objective account of any incident, the UAW invited clergymen, reporters, and representatives of civil-liberties groups to be
108 bystanders.

Richard Frankensteen (left) and Walter Reuther (second from right) announce the campaign to organize Ford

About an hour before the shifts changed at mid-afternoon on May 26, 1937, Reuther, Frankensteen, several other UAW members, and the Reverend Raymond P. Sanford climbed the steps of an overpass that linked the Rouge with a parking lot. The group posed briefly for newspaper photographers, an action that seemed to energize loiterers along the edge of the overpass. Some of these men moved toward the journalists and others toward Frankensteen and Reuther. "This is Ford property," someone said. "Get the hell off of here." The UAW delegates obediently turned back toward the stairs, while behind them a scuffle began as photographers defended their cameras. Within a few steps, the fight overtook Reuther and Frankensteen, who were worked over professionally. Four or five thugs

The "Battle of the Overpass"

isolated Frankensteen, a burly former football player, lifted his coat over his head to bind his arms, and punched, kicked, gouged, and stomped him before pushing him down the stairs. "It was," Frankensteen remarked that evening, "the most ruthless fight I have ever been in. They not only knock you down, but kick you and jump on you."

Walter Reuther had a similar experience, and other UAW members, male and female, at other gates received equally rude receptions. Women were verbally abused, had leaflets wrenched from their hands and their arms twisted, and were slammed into departing streetcars. One woman, Reverend Sanford said, "was kicked in the stomach, and vomited at my feet"; the incident tore a pleading "You mustn't hurt these women" from a watching Dearborn policeman. A union member attempting to help received a broken back for his chivalry. A young black man sustained several blows to the head in spite of instructions shouted to his attackers to "Hit him in the stomach; hell, you can't hurt a nigger when you hit him over the

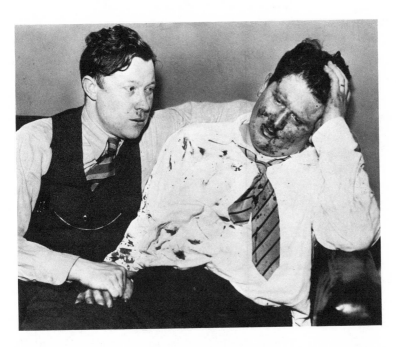

head." Another man was being beaten in an office in the plant until a fastidious executive suggested that the task be completed somewhere else.[20]

Harry Bennett chose to ignore that incident as well as other accounts of witnesses not in his employ: "Our Servicemen had absolute orders not to interfere with the distribution of pamphlets," Bennett said. Whatever their orders, servicemen chased reporters and photographers, confiscated notes and film, and attempted to suppress photographs that later identified members of the security force who assaulted Frankensteen and Reuther. When subpoenaed, Bennett blandly denied all and suggested prosecution of the UAW for trespass. When the National Labor Relations Board (NLRB) probed the incident, the company challenged the board's jurisdiction. When the NLRB found that Ford had "deliberately planned and carried out the assaults in an effort to crush union organization," Henry Ford himself dismissed the allegation out of hand. "Anybody who knows the Ford Motor Company," he said, "knows that the

111

things the Board charged never happened and could not happen here."[21]

Ford's rigid resistance evoked considerable support from working people who worried that a closed shop might shut them out and that sit-down strikes might lead to fundamental change. Dozens of letters to the Detroit press referred to UAW officials as grafters who "finally got what was coming to them" and then, like "cry babies," tattled to the federal government. Other people had rights too: Ford had property rights, and nonunion employees had a right to their jobs. "There is not an automobile factory in Detroit," one person wrote in defiance of facts, "where employment is as steady and wages as good as at Ford's."

> It is the foreign element that is doing all this kicking. Let them go back to their native land if they don't like it here.

Henry Ford, protested another correspondent, was engaged in a patriotic effort to "keep Russia across the world."[22]

The "battle of the overpass," Homer Martin prophesied, would give "tremendous impetus" to the UAW's effort to organize Ford. In fact, the drive stalled, partly because the nation's economic recovery also stalled. Industrial payrolls fell nearly 25 percent in the last half of 1937, and industrial production declined even more sharply. By January 1938, General Motors had furloughed 60 percent of the work force, and most of the rest worked less than half-time. In January, only one in eight Ford employees had full-time employment. The expected surge of spring sales never came; automobile production in 1938 was only half that for 1937.

And the New Deal stalled too. Congress became more conservative, more wary of Roosevelt's direction. Nineteen thirty-eight was no rerun of 1932, to be sure: in spite of the economy's decline, for instance, unions remained incomparably stronger than they had been before Roosevelt's inauguration. Yet neither the unions, nor the Roosevelt administration that had fostered them, regarded the closing months of the decade as a propitious time to push ahead.

Not until late in 1940 did the UAW renew the test with Ford. Following an intensive recruiting drive, the union asked the NLRB to hold a collective-bargaining election at the Rouge. Harry Bennett followed Henry Ford's script to the end. "We will bargain," Bennett blustered, "until hell freezes over, but they won't get anything." He alternately wooed and harassed shop stewards in an effort to divide and confuse the union. He reminded Detroit's blacks that Ford had hired them when others would not, and he asked their vote against the union in return. In April, when the UAW converted a spontaneous walkout into a strike, more than a thousand blacks, under Bennett's direction, remained inside the Rouge.

Although Bennett had misled his corps of black strikebreakers, there was logic behind the loyalty many blacks felt for Ford. If the UAW officially condemned discrimination, black auto workers nevertheless felt the unofficial prejudice of individual union members and heard the racist muttering along the picket line; Detroit's unions had traditionally segregated those black workers who were permitted to join. If Franklin Roosevelt had wooed black voters, his New Deal had given them little in return. Yet Henry Ford had at least offered blacks jobs, however menial and undesirable, for which many in Detroit's black community were grateful. When gratitude among the black strikebreakers wore thin, Bennett's security force simply forbade their departure.

But there were too few strikebreakers to resume production. Bennett finally agreed to permit the NLRB to hold an election in May 1941, in return for the board's willingness to postpone hearings that seemed likely to reveal the seamy side of Ford's security service. Given a secret ballot, seven of ten Ford workers selected the UAW, and most of the others the AFL. Only about 3 percent of Henry Ford's 80,000 employees vindicated his reiterated faith that his workers would never choose a union. Bennett conceded with his customary grace: it was, he said, "a great victory for the Communist party."[23]

The battle over, the Ford Motor Company surrendered more completely than had General Motors or Chrysler. The River Rouge became a closed shop, and Henry Ford, the paternalistic champion of nonunion labor, collected dues for the UAW. He raised wages to correspond to those competitors paid and accepted seniority rights,   113 overtime schedules, and other provisions that would have been inconceivable a year earlier. When the contract was ready, Ford had second thoughts and vowed to shut the Rouge before he would sign. But his vows, like his predictions, were at a discount; Mrs. Ford made him change his mind, he later told a puzzled associate who had taken him at his word.

Maybe Mrs. Ford was indeed responsible. But the Wagner Act too had had something to do with Ford's decision, for the NLRB had begun to air some of the company's dirtiest laundry, and any further evasion of the law risked contempt of court. However erratic Ford's behavior after a stroke and more than seventy-five years, he knew that his slice of automobile sales, once incomparably the largest, was in 1940 the smallest of the three major firms. Bad publicity and prolonged labor trouble would not enlarge his 20 percent of the market. And the federal government, whatever Ford thought of it, would become every company's largest customer if the United States entered the European war. Already Ford had lost a large federal order for trucks partly because the government disapproved of his labor policy. Industrial change in the twentieth century owed much to Henry Ford. Some of the progress he had set in motion at last had caught him from behind.

EXPLOSIONS—AT HOME AND ABROAD

New Deal programs designed to stimulate prosperity through governmental spending had less impact in Detroit than later appropriations to win the war. Through 1939 and 1940, federal officials hesitated to prepare for American participation. When participation seemed imminent, in order to make up lost time, they relied on firms with the industrial expertise and productive capacity to provide vast quantities of goods at great speed. For vehicles and engines and a host of related products, procurement officers sent contracts to Detroit. Although no New Dealer deliberately planned to enhance the competitive position of the business executives Roosevelt had once denounced as "economic royalists," by 1940 the hundred largest manufacturers produced 30 percent of the nation's

Wartime Detroit: plenty of good jobs

output; by 1943 their proportion approached 70 percent and was rising.

Production created jobs, and workers had to go where the industrial giants were. Between 1940 and 1943, almost 500,000 people moved to Detroit, where newcomers had great difficulty locating any place to live. One in two black families and one in seven whites in Detroit occupied substandard housing. Workers at Willow Run, the new aircraft factory Ford was building west of Detroit, lived in tents and trailers, without zoning or sanitation codes, "in unrelieved fear," one historian has written, "of fire and epidemic."[24]

The lack of housing was but one example of the shortage of consumer goods. American civilians complained about shortages

Temporary housing for a family of four: Detroit, 1942

and rationing and governmental regulations, even though they lived far more comfortably than people in other countries and, in many cases, better than they had themselves lived during the depression. The grumbling was often good natured and usually informed by the realization that "there's a war on." But the regimentation, the crowding, the pressure to produce, the lack of amenities, and the relentless fact of the war itself made for irritable individuals, bickering families, tense communities. Money, even when plentiful, was an inadequate social lubricant because neither goods nor satisfaction were in the marketplace. Money did not replace a father in the service or a mother on the afternoon shift. Money could not buy a new car or leisurely travel or a house in the suburbs. Money could not shut off the war for a week and allow frayed nerves to mend.

For black Americans, discrimination made it all worse. They could sweep and serve and join segregated battalions. They could stay on Southern farms or pile up in Northern ghettoes, where rents were exorbitant and the infant mortality rate about double that for whites. They could accept second-class treatment and racial slurs, or they could protest and be accused of subverting national unity in wartime. They could not expect much help from the federal government, which ranked racial justice well down on the nation's wartime agenda. The Fair Employment Practices Commission (FEPC), Roosevelt's gesture toward equal opportunity, had little budget and only the cancellation of federal contracts as a means of coercing discriminatory employers. Since the government wanted production more than reform, the sanction was rarely invoked.

Wartime Detroit had neither an atmosphere nor a heritage of toleration. The thriving Ku Klux Klan chapter of the 1920s changed form but not substance and survived through the 1930s and into the 1940s. The German-American Bund, whose tinpot *führer* had been on Ford's payroll, was only more blatantly anti-Semitic than some other ethnic societies. Both Ford and Father Charles Coughlin, the Detroit priest whose Sunday afternoon broadcasts gave him a nationwide parish, had publicized the *Protocols of the Elders of Zion,* a forgery purporting to outline a Jewish plot to dominate the world. A host of "improvement associations" coordinated vigilante activity to keep blacks out of white neighborhoods.

One segment of Detroit's black community expressed its resentment of discrimination through the National Association for the Advancement of Colored People (NAACP). The Detroit chapter of the organization, 20,000 strong, was one of the nation's largest. It sponsored a rally in the spring of 1943, at which thousands shouted their approval of the "Cadillac Charter," which called for an end to discrimination. Two months later, the national NAACP held an emergency convention in Detroit to underline the demand for equality. The Detroit chapter actively pressed for more and better housing for blacks and protested segregated federal housing in the city and at Willow Run. But there was not much result of the effort.

Some of the city's blacks needed no organization to express their resentment. In crowded public buildings, parks, and buses, they traded racial insults with whites and sometimes initiated the exchange. Young black men cut seats in movie theaters, and sometimes one another, with three- and four-inch knives. "We could do without a lot of clowning in public," a columnist in one of Detroit's black newspapers wrote, without the knives, without "filthy language," and without "acting as if we owned the whole world."[25]

In another context, that sort of conduct was called "juvenile delinquency," which was not, of course, unique to blacks. No ethnic group held a monopoly on truancy, theft, vandalism, venereal disease, or any other index of restless, or even alienated, youth. The nation's preoccupation with courage and strength could make the normal combative impulses of adolescent males seem patriotic; with a racial focus, those same fighting qualities led to incidents. The conventional metaphor for this mixture was dynamite, and explosions occurred in 1943 in shipyards in Mobile, Alabama, and Chester, Pennsylvania; in Harlem, after a rumor that a white policeman had killed a black soldier; and in Los Angeles, where white servicemen and young Mexican-Americans clashed over "zoot suits" and girls.

Observers anxiously monitored the racial situation in Detroit, where conditions seemed especially conducive to a riot that might create industrial chaos. The city might "blow up Hitler," *Life* magazine reported in 1942, "or . . . blow up the U.S." A federal agency warned that "hell is going to be let loose" unless there was "strong and quick intervention, . . . preferably by the President."[26] To Detroit's long history of industrial violence was added the war's constant emphasis on violence; to the long tradition of racial hostility were added the amplified messages of merchants of bigotry; to the usual stress of urban living was added the presence of disoriented newcomers for whom there was no place; and to the normal abrasive energy of youth was added a new independence promoted by money, inattentive parents, and ineffective social control. Early in June 1943, Walter White, the executive secretary of the NAACP, decided to say publicly "what has been whispered throughout Detroit for months." A race riot, White feared, "may break out here at any time."[27]

Indeed there had been one the year before at the opening of Sojourner Truth Homes, a federal housing project that appeared to enlarge the black district. Whites protested, at first politically and then with stones and clubs in February 1942, when blacks attempted to occupy their new quarters. Federal officials hesitated and betrayed a willingness to sell the blacks out, but the municipal

118

government stood by them. With the assistance of the state militia, black tenants eventually occupied their new, but still segregated, apartments.

That result was no settlement, and racial antagonism intensified during the next year. When black families bought houses in a white district, parading Klansmen smashed the windows; when police provided ineffective protection, armed black homeowners announced that they were ready to protect themselves. An argument over the use of a punching bag at Eastwood Park eventually required tear gas and reinforcements from the state police. Twenty-five thousand white workers at Packard Motors walked off their jobs when three blacks received the promotions that their seniority and the union's contract required. Better that the nation's enemies should win the war, some of the strikers remarked, than that black workers should work on the line. Uniformed white men and young black civilians tangled constantly; one confrontation soon involved several hundred brawlers.[28]

Every incident seemed to stiffen the resolve of black leaders. The *Michigan Chronicle* and local black spokesmen echoed the determination of the *Pittsburgh Courier* and other national voices that were determined to use the war to advance racial justice. If war created economic opportunities, they must not be lost; if propaganda required denunciation of racial discrimination, white Americans must listen too; if blacks were to make a full contribution to the war effort, they must become full citizens as well. "We may have to fight another war in this country after the present war is over," Adam Clayton Powell, the Harlem editor, clergyman, and politician, told an audience in Detroit. Returning black soldiers would not slink back "to a sharecropper's cabin without a fight," and they would not accept "pie in the sky" instead of "ribs and grits . . . [and a] Federal housing project right here and now."[29]

That was the sort of militance that worried William Dowling, the Wayne County prosecutor. He encountered dozens of racial incidents in the course of a week's business; some of them, he thought, could have been avoided if black leaders had preached patience instead of rebellion. Had Dowling simultaneously condemned the militance of white racists, he might have secured a more receptive black audience. Instead, his "asinine" remarks became for the *Chronicle* one more piece of evidence that the city's law enforcement agencies were in league with the interests blocking black progress.[30]

There was initially no way to distinguish what became known as *the* Detroit riot of 1943 from other racial incidents before and after. It looked at first like one more fuse leading toward that powder keg. On the afternoon of Sunday, June 20, perhaps 100,000 people thronged the park on Belle Isle—canoeing, swimming, picnicking, and otherwise seeking relief from the steamy heat of early summer. Because Belle Isle was not far from Paradise Valley, much of the crowd was black—about 85 percent of it, William Dowling later wrote in an overestimate that would have placed half of the city's black population on the island. Young blacks who had been shoved around a few days before at another park found some whites to shove back. Pushing and discourtesy became something of a group pastime in the lines that formed at food stands, toilets, and recreational facilities. Police received reports of minor altercations throughout the afternoon and into the evening. After midnight, however, the fights seemed to disappear with the thinning crowds, and police thought they had weathered the storm.

Like summer lightning, the storm simply skipped on. The crowd from Belle Isle dispersed all over the city, carrying accounts and bruises from the battle, and rumors as if they were facts. The story that energized white mobs began with an imagined rape; the counterpart in the black community began with a murder that never took place. At a night club about three miles from Belle Isle, somebody shouted that whites at the park had killed a mother and her baby. Several hundred blacks pushed out of the Forest Club into the street, where they began to stone whites in passing cars. Before dawn the mob was smashing windows up and down Hastings Street, the main street of Paradise Valley. Busy protecting property in the ghetto, Detroit's police offered little protection when whites began harassing blacks outside it.

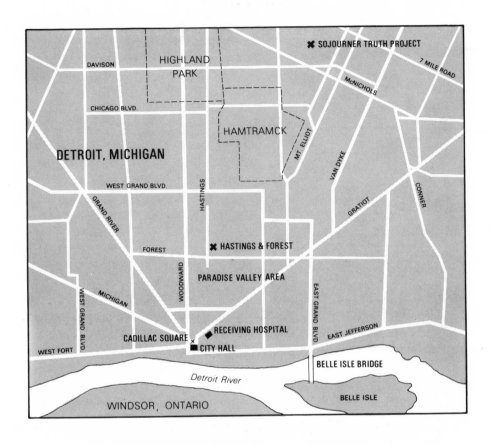

DETROIT, MICHIGAN

Before dawn on Monday morning police and city officials mistook a lull for the end and decided they would not need outside assistance. By mid-morning, they had reversed themselves, and Mayor Edward Jeffries informed Governor Harry F. Kelly that Detroit was out of control. That telephone call opened an elaborate political quadrille, as state, city, and federal authorities maneuvered to avoid criticism. Hours slipped by while troops waited for the mayor and the governor formally to request federal help, a step they hoped not to take because it might later seem a confession of their own

Woodward Avenue, June 21, 1943

inadequacy. Federal authorities, including the President, were reluctant to use the army against civilians until all the legal niceties had been satisfied. When every face had been saved, federal troops stopped the riot in an hour and a half and kept the peace—or, more accurately, kept disorder subdued—in the tense months that followed.

Meanwhile, thirty-four people died and hundreds were injured. The property damage was reparable, though the reputation of the police in the black community was not. The interruption in defense production was temporary. But bayonets were as useless in mending Detroit's social fabric as they had been for weaving cloth in Lawrence more than thirty years before. The sullen, patched-up peace temporarily concealed intolerance and division and hate. Or, more likely, the memory of forty-eight hours of terror kept recurring incidents from igniting the dynamite once more.

For almost everyone in the city carried a personal collection of mental snapshots of anarchy:

- Hastings Street on June 22, the sidewalk glistening with glass, the debris of looters in the gutter, the dismembered mannequins from a clothing store suggesting a macabre cartoon no artist had the stomach to draw.
- The bench at receiving hospital, where a puzzled black man mused with equally puzzled whites on either side of him about why the mob had picked them out.
- The enterprising looter who established an open-air discount house, and his confederate who provided baskets for the convenience of those who had neglected to steal their own.
- The sixteen-year-old who went out with his buddies to have "some fun shooting niggers." He killed one—a middle-aged man waiting for a streetcar—and talked about the exploit in jail. "My blood was boiling," the lad recalled, and he would "probably do it again" if he thought he "wouldn't get caught." He supposed he would go to jail, though he would have preferred "to go to Italy and kill me some Italians," he said, displaying the American flag tattooed on his arm. He was sorry for his mother,

123

who had "always told [him] to be a good boy." He was sorry for his girl friend, who seemed to have gone to Cleveland. But he apparently felt no sorrow for the family of his victim.[31]

The sorrow of Michigan's public officials seemed curiously misplaced too. They regretted the lapse in war production and the disclosure that racial rifts marred wartime unity. But they decided not to compound chagrin with careful investigation. No official body asked why policemen shot eighteen of twenty-five dead blacks and none of the nine dead whites. The Detroit City Council voted down the mayor's half-hearted request for a grand jury. There was no serious probe of the tragic delay in sending for federal troops. The investigative committee Governor Kelly appointed consisted of Detroit's police commissioner, the Wayne County prosecutor, the head of the state police, and the state's attorney general—all men with a personal stake in the report's conclusions.

Hastings Street

Aftermath

Their report blamed the blacks, a thesis that William Dowling, the principal author, had advanced previously. "Who constantly beats the drums of 'racial prejudice, inequality, intolerance, [and] discrimination,'" Dowling asked, and who "challenges . . . hoodlum elements to rise against this alleged oppression?" The answer, for Dowling, was "many so-called responsible Negro leaders," who had urged their followers to be "'militant' in the struggle for racial equality." His investigation found no excessive use of force by police, no abuse of authority. All eighteen victims of police bullets were listed as justifiable homicides. Governor Kelly called the document "a completely factual report" that required "no further action." Dowling had swept the riot under the rug, and Kelly resolutely kept it there.[32]

Protests were unavailing. R. J. Thomas, president of the United Auto Workers, called Dowling's remarks "the most serious incitation to race riots we have had since the race riots themselves." If the prosecutor had any evidence for his condemnation of black leaders, Thomas continued, a grand jury ought to hear it. And perhaps

125

investigate the "deplorable stupidity and callousness" of police as well, the paper of the usually moderate Urban League added. The editor of the *Michigan Chronicle* conceded that black leaders might have aroused the interest of rank-and-file blacks in equality. But who, he asked, stirred up the whites to refuse to grant it? The authorities, the editor continued, seemed "very sure that the Negro leaders who preach equality and ask that democracy work right here in Detroit are responsible for making the Negroes fighting mad, but the white mobsters just got fighting mad by accident." The *Chronicle* pointed out the report's omissions: "hate strikes, slums, jim crow practices, police brutality, the infringement of our civil liberties" were among them—and compared the document to Hitler's arguments that Jews were to blame for Nazi pogroms.[33]

Some of the unofficial explanations were no more perceptive than Dowling's. A newspaper in Jackson, Mississippi, attributed the riot to Eleanor Roosevelt, who had encouraged blacks to become insolent. The *Detroit News* and several of its correspondents blamed newcomers of both races, who brought "their ingrained resentments and ignorant prejudice" with them, and were ill prepared for the city's racial tolerance and "the sudden prosperity of war wages." The data on arrests showed that outsiders were no more responsible than Eleanor Roosevelt. About three of four of those arrested had lived in Detroit more than five years. Most were war workers with steady employment and good wages. They were young, married men—the sort of people who personified the city's future.[34]

Paul Taylor worried about that. "Funny how we look every place for the cause of the riot except right here," he wrote the editor of the *Detroit News.* "Every one of us knows that the cause is race prejudice and that every one of us by his attitude or indifference has contributed to it." That prejudice was "bad enough without adding intellectual dishonesty and hypocrisy" to it. The fault, Taylor concluded with an assist from Shakespeare, "lies not in our stars but in ourselves."[35]

William Dowling demonstrably lacked that insight. If he had realized his racist assumptions, he surely would have concealed

126

them more tactfully. Nor was Dowling the only victim of this unconscious prejudice. Roosevelt's attorney general, Francis Biddle, suggested after the riot that the President use his war powers to halt the migration of blacks to Detroit and other urban centers that "cannot absorb them, either on account of their physical limitations or cultural background." Roosevelt's response revealed presidential confusion about cause and effect, for he deplored the divisions the riots produced. The nation's leaders, from county prosecutor to President, apparently could not, as well as would not, see their own bias. Under those circumstances, they could hardly educate the electorate to tolerance.

Detroit had no patent on wartime discrimination and blacks no exclusive right to rage. The army packed Japanese-Americans off to relocation centers where isolation was as official as Southern segregation and more confining. On another level, individual Americans believed that tax courts, ration boards, and the selective service system had treated them outrageously. The multiple anxieties of women ordinarily found a private expression, but sometimes burst into public indignation. In a sense, it was anger—not only the patriotic anger generated against the nation's foes but also the constructive anger generated by reminders of crisis and exhortations to sacrifice—that animated the entire population, at home and in uniform.

Anger found an outlet in violence—the destructive violence of a race riot and war, the ritualized violence of frenzied production, the psychological violence of a disintegrating family, the internal violence that warped individual personalities. Neither anger nor violence is unique to war, a fact too often ignored while the battle continued. Even the return of peace could not warm every family circle, cure youthful delinquency, or enlighten racial bigots. Some of these "wartime problems" remained to trouble postwar America. But at least they were problems associated with prosperity, fundamentally different from those that had plagued Detroit, and the nation, during a decade of depression.

127

Notes

[1] The fullest scholarly account of the "hunger march" is that of Alex Baskin, "The Ford Hunger March—1932," in *Labor History*, Summer 1972, p. 331ff. Events may also be followed in the *Detroit News* and the *Detroit Free Press*, and in national reform journals, including the *New Republic* and *Nation*. Other versions include Sidney Fine, *Frank Murphy: The Detroit Years* (Ann Arbor: University of Michigan Press, 1975), Keith Sward, *The Legend of Henry Ford* (New York: Rinehart, 1948), Richard D. Lunt, *The High Ministry of Government* (Detroit: Wayne State University Press, 1965), and Robert Conot, *American Odyssey* (New York: William Morrow, 1974).

[2] *Monthly Labor Review*, June 1930, pp. 11–54.

[3] Charles R. Walker, "Down and Out in Detroit," in *Forum*, September 1931, p. 129.

[4] Barney Nagler, *Brown Bomber* (New York: World, 1972), p. 20.

[5] Walker, "Down and Out . . . ," pp. 130–31.

[6] Fine, *Murphy*, p. 215.

[7] *Ibid.*, p. 251; see also *Commonweal*, August 19, 1931, p. 378, and *Survey*, January 15, 1931, p. 419.

[8] Walker, "Down and Out . . . ," p. 131.

[9] Fine, *Murphy*, p. 257; *Monthly Labor Review*, April 1931, p. 27; J. Woodford Howard, *Mr. Justice Murphy* (Princeton: Princeton University Press, 1968), p. 37.

[10] Fine, *Murphy*, pp. 249–50; *Detroit Free Press*, February 11, 1932.

[11] *New York Times*, June 2, 1932; Fine, *Murphy*, pp. 349–50; Howard, *Murphy*, p. 52.

[12] James T. Patterson, *The New Deal and the States* (Princeton: Princeton University Press, 1969), p. 126; see also volume II of *The New Deal*, edited by John Braeman, Robert H. Bremner, and David Brody (Columbus: Ohio State University Press, 1975).

[13] The strike in Flint is covered by Sidney Fine, *Sit-Down* (Ann Arbor: University of Michigan Press, 1969).

[14] Except where otherwise noted, this account of the sit-down strikes in Detroit is based on coverage in the *Detroit News*, March 1937.

[15] *Detroit News*, March 16, 1937.

[16] Mary Heaton Vorse, "Detroit Has the Jitters," in *New Republic*, April 7, 1937, p. 256; see also *Business Week*, March 27, 1937, p. 13.

[17] Quoted in Howard, *Murphy*, p. 153.

[18] *Detroit News*, April 7, 1937.

[19] *Ibid.*, April 8, 10, 14, 1937; *Business Week*, June 26, 1937, p. 18; *Time*, April 19, 1937, p. 16.

[20] National Labor Relations Board, *Hearings . . .* (Washington: Government Printing Office, 1938), vol. IV, pp. 633, 635; vol. XIV (1940), p. 362; *Detroit News*, May 27, 1937.

[21] Allan Nevins and Frank Ernest Hill, *Ford: Decline and Rebirth* (New York: Scribner, 1963), vol. II, p. 141.

[22] *Detroit News*, May 30, 1937.

[23] Sward, *Legend*, pp. 417–18.

[24] Richard Polenburg, *War and Society* (Philadelphia: Lippincott, 1972), p. 114.

[25] *Michigan Chronicle,* March 13, 1943; May 22, 29, 1943; June 19, 1943.

[26] *Life,* August 17, 1943, p. 15; Harvard Sitkoff, "The Detroit Race Riot of 1943," in *Michigan History,* Autumn 1969, p. 187.

[27] Quoted in Sitkoff, "Detroit Race Riot," p. 188.

[28] *Michigan Chronicle,* April 10, 1943; June 19, 1943; *Detroit News,* June 5, 14, 16, 1943.

[29] *Detroit News,* May 30, 1943.

[30] *Michigan Chronicle,* June 19, 1943 (editorial).

[31] *Ibid.,* June 26, 1943; *Detroit News,* June 21, 22, 1943; August 1, 1943.

[32] *Detroit News,* August 11, 1943.

[33] Alfred M. Lee and Norman D. Humphrey, *Race Riot* (New York: Dryden Press, 1943), p. 137; *Michigan Chronicle,* July 3, 1943; August 21, 1943.

[34] *Michigan Chronicle,* July 3, 1943; *Detroit News,* June 22, 23, 26, 1943; August 11, 1943.

[35] *Detroit News,* June 30, 1943.

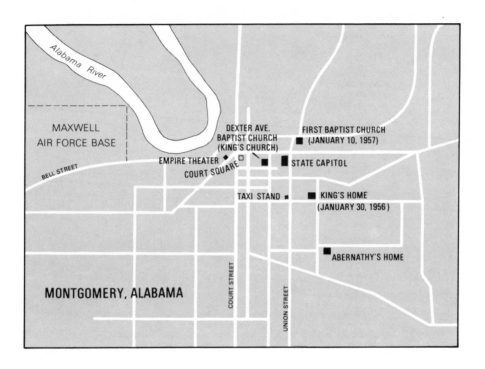

MONTGOMERY, ALABAMA

Peaceful Souls
and Tired Feet:
Montgomery, 1955

4

Martin Luther King, Jr., did not always arise with the sun. But Monday, December 5, 1955, was a special day, and the excited young minister could not sleep. Impatiently he paced the house, waiting for the first bus of the day to reach its stop near his front porch. The vehicle was usually crowded with black domestics on their way to the kitchens and yards of the white employers of Montgomery, Alabama; it would be a good test of the boycott he and others had urged local blacks to undertake. King had prepared himself for disappointment and hoped to be cheered by partial success. But the first bus was empty, and the second, and the third. The exhilarated pastor undertook a wider investigation in his car.

In another part of the city, a young white reporter was conducting his own investigation. Joe Azbell, city editor of the *Montgomery Advertiser*, stood on Court Square in the dim dawn. The city's Christmas decorations caught the early sun and tinkled when they stirred. A banner proclaiming PEACE ON EARTH cast a shadow, through which an erect, middle-aged black man walked as he crossed the street. At the corner a bus stopped, and the driver opened the door. When the man did not move, the driver asked "Are you gettin' on?" "I ain't gettin' on," the black returned, "'till Jim Crow gets off." Jim Crow—the personification of racial segregation—was a perpetual passenger, so the driver closed the door and drove off.

The struggle to get Jim Crow off the buses and out of American life was one of the central themes of the nation's history after the Second World War. In retrospect, the early stages of the civil rights movement may seem idealistic and naive, and the participation of Northern whites patronizing and hypocritical. The progress they celebrated seems trivial now that Americans have a somewhat better sense of the detours on their pilgrimage to equality. Yet President Harry Truman's order in 1948 ending segregation in the armed forces was no minor matter when much of the nation's male youth expected a tour of military duty. And the Supreme Court's unanimous ruling in 1954 against segregated schooling in the case of *Oliver Brown et al.* v. *Board of Education of Topeka, Kansas* was even more inclusive.

President Dwight Eisenhower subordinated racial reform to his primary concern with domestic calm. He hoped to heal social divisions that derived from Truman's controversial domestic and foreign policies, to end the frustrating Korean War, to take the passion out of the nation's obsession with subversion. Eisenhower soothed the country by his evident and sincere affirmation of traditional verities—patriotism, public service, personal courtesy, free enterprise. Southern whites found his stance in the middle of the political road as congenial as his silent acceptance of continued segregation. Temperamentally, the President was neither a bigot nor a crusader, and his administration needed the political help of Southerners who dominated Congress. Pressure to carry out the *Brown* decision had to come from outside Washington.

And not, in most instances, from whites, since any affirmation of racial equality tended to provoke a noisy defense of white supremacy that forced moderates to choose between black and white. Even well-intentioned whites ordinarily kept a prudent silence in order to maintain their standing in the white community. When cornered, Southern officials declared that the *Brown* ruling applied only to the schools of Topeka and required no change in local laws or habits. This do-nothing strategy of whites gave the initiative to Southern blacks, who began to ask admission to schools and all the other places from which they had always been excluded.

It became customary to identify the leaders of these efforts as "new Negroes," a phrase that often implied Northern education, Northern residence, or extensive contact with whites through military service or another profession. This identification betrayed, slightly more subtly, the same condescension white Southerners expressed when they damned "outside agitators" for racial friction. Both explanations assumed that Southern blacks could not themselves conceive and execute a strategy for integration without assistance from whites, from an "enlightened" organization like the National Association for the Advancement of Colored People (NAACP), or from a subversive one such as the Communist party. A black mailman in Montgomery knew better:

> New Negro? It's just us old Negroes, the same old folks. It's not the "new Negro"—it's the new times.[1]

In many respects, the postwar years were in fact "new times" in the Old South. Diversified and mechanized agriculture reduced the region's dependence on cotton and sharecropping. Displaced tenant farmers had to seek new jobs in cities—in Detroit or Chicago or Los Angeles, or in the industries and service trades of expanding Southern cities. Urban blacks gradually discovered that concentration gave them an independence that rural isolation never bestowed. In cities, blacks could support and encourage one another, gain the leverage of their combined economic power, and bring pressure to conform on those who were ready to sell out too soon.

Most urban whites retained their sentimental attachment to the Old South; the Stars and Bars, the flag of the Confederacy, still flew over the state capitol in Montgomery, for instance, and the city proudly billed itself as "the cradle of the Confederacy." But economically, Montgomery had rejoined the Union, for national defense was the chief industry. More important than the marketing of beef or lumber, and more important than the production of fertilizer for Alabama's farms were the air bases located just out of town. One in seven families in the region depended upon the sixty million federal dollars that flowed through Maxwell Field. Except for a few local peculiarities, wrote a visitor from the North in 1956, Montgomery could pass for Hartford or Des Moines.[2]

One of those peculiarities, of course, was Montgomery's race relations. However rigid the segregation of Hartford or Des Moines, the pattern was not frozen in law. Even the federal government's insistence on the integration of Maxwell Field had almost no impact on Montgomery. A municipal ordinance, for example, prescribed separate taxis for black and white, and drivers who brought servicemen of both races from the base to the city were arrested and fined. Commanders at the base made no effort to modify off-post segregation and ordered air force personnel to avoid involvement when the boycott created racial tension in Montgomery.[3]

Statistics indicate the persistence of injustice. The median white worker earned almost twice the $970 annual wage of the median black in 1950. Almost two-thirds of the employed black women were domestic servants, and almost half the black men were

134

unskilled laborers or domestic handymen; there were two black lawyers in Alabama's capital city, where white lawyers abounded. Two of three black families lacked flush toilets, a statistic that would have chagrined the city fathers of Lawrence forty years earlier. Systematic discrimination kept about fourteen of fifteen potential black voters unregistered and prevented any political expression of discontent.[4]

The habits of segregation lingered in the decade after the Second World War, and the absence of new modes of race relations sometimes made social contact awkward. If black policemen were appointed, could they arrest white people? Should the white sales attendant say "thank you, sir" to a black customer? Could any step be taken that would not lead to integrated schools and to "race-mixing"? One of Montgomery's Episcopal clergymen explained the dilemma in terms of broken communication. Although we know the blacks we live with, Thomas R. Thrasher wrote, "we are aware that we know them not." "They speak," he continued; "we do not understand."[5]

Many white moderates, like Thomas Thrasher, acknowledged the need to modify segregated ways. But most whites reserved the right to specify both kind and quantity of reform. "You'll be surprised at all the things we're planning for you people," Montgomery's mayor remarked to the young black lawyer who sought desegregation of the city's parks. The mayor probably meant well, but he could neither give blacks what they asked nor concede their ability to plan for themselves.[6]

Actually, there were blacks in Montgomery who were entirely capable of planning for themselves. E. D. Nixon, a scarred veteran of the civil rights struggle, had registered to vote, run for municipal office, held virtually every office in the local NAACP, and served as president of the Alabama chapter. Mrs. Jo Ann Robinson, a teacher at the local black college and head of the Women's Political Caucus, had planned a bus boycott once before and cancelled it because the unmarried, pregnant, fifteen-year-old who had been arrested seemed an unsuitable symbol of racial discrimination. Ralph Abernathy, the sensible pastor of the First Baptist Church, counseled his friend

Martin Luther King, Jr., and sometimes helped stiffen his determination.

King himself had some of the qualifications of an "outside agitator." Educated in the North and recently arrived in Montgomery, King's roots were nonetheless in the South. The son and grandson of Atlanta ministers, King had been reared in relative comfort among proud, educated blacks. His mother's father had sparked a black boycott that contributed to the failure of the Hearst paper in Atlanta. Martin Luther King, Sr., did not let success obscure his origin on a sharecropper's patch, his struggle for education, or his anger over Georgia's segregation statutes. He insulated his son from some of the ugliest manifestations of racism and encouraged the youngster's bookishness. Young Martin entered Morehouse College at fifteen and, after graduation, went to theological school in Pennsylvania and then sought further graduate study at Boston University. King could have made his career in the North, but the South was home and in 1954 he and his wife moved into the parsonage of Montgomery's Dexter Avenue Baptist Church.

Martin Luther King, Jr., and Coretta Scott King on steps of Dexter Avenue Baptist Church; Alabama state capitol in background.

In his first year in Montgomery, King attended to his pastoral chores and completed his doctoral dissertation. Although he declined to become president of the local chapter of the NAACP, justifiably pleading inadequate time, he hoped to persuade his parish to support programs for social and political change.

While King learned his calling and his community, the people of Alabama began to assimilate the Supreme Court's ruling on desegregation. A federal judge ordered the state university to admit two black women whose request had been in the courts for years. Parents in several communities, including Montgomery, petitioned school boards to assign black children to white schools. E. D. Nixon, head of the NAACP's committee on education, suggested a biracial committee to plan desegregation. The school board denied the petition and authorized, but did not appoint, the committee. Although the superintendent thought a great deal of study would be required, he did not indicate when it might begin. The *Montgomery Advertiser* approved evasion as the only possible course. The city would maintain segregation "pending, of course, a committee report and perhaps two or three exhaustive subcommittee reports."[7]

White supremacists found the *Advertiser*'s support for segregation too tepid. The paper reported formation of die-hard White Citizens' Councils (WCC) in Mississippi and elsewhere in Alabama, but frowned editorially at the old-fashioned racism of these "manicured Ku Kluxers." An Alabama state senator suggested that a refusal to subscribe and to advertise might persuade the editors to reenlist in "this fight to preserve our heritage of segregation." A correspondent picked up the suggestion of economic coercion and carried it several steps further: all employers should fire their black employees and all businesses deny blacks credit.[8]

Economic pressure was the tactic White Citizens' Councils advocated, and the *Advertiser* assigned a reporter to ask Montgomery's whites their opinion of the organization. The reporter found cautious support for the WCC's purpose, but not much for economic coercion, a conclusion confirmed in October when disappointed sponsors conceded that only 300 of Montgomery's 70,000 whites had attended the WCC's organizational rally. The audience, the

Advertiser noted editorially, was not only pathetically tiny but also unrepresentative of the community: there were "no face cards"—"no bankers, doctors, lawyers, merchants, insurance executives, contractors, architects, PTA officers, preachers, auto dealers, gasoline distributors or—conspicuously—politicians . . . within a mile of the meeting." And what the audience heard were tired clichés about "mongrelizing our race."

The rejoinder was measured and literate. A letter to the editor corrected the *Advertiser*'s mistaken report that no clergymen had attended the WCC meeting. But Chester E. Johnson accepted the *Advertiser*'s general thesis that the community's leaders disdained the WCC, a circumstance that he thought augured well for the organization. Leaders, Johnson argued, had failed effectively to uphold the nation's principles during negotiations with Stalin at Yalta and in the United Nations; leaders had reduced the nation to its present sorry state. The WCC wanted no leaders and relied instead on the ordinary people who were the country's greatest resource.[9]

Foremost among the leaders Alabama's WCC distrusted was Governor James E. Folsom. Called "Big Jim" because of his stature and "Kissing Jim" because of his campaign technique, Folsom had been the state's governor from 1947–1951 and easily won a second term in 1954. He was, the editor of the *Advertiser* wrote, "the only major southern demagogue in our history, with the short-time exception of Tom Watson of Georgia, who has . . . been able to harness the so-called red necks and the colored voters." Keeping those discordant factions "very happily in the same vest pocket," Grover Hall continued, was "an extraordinary performance in American politics."[10] Folsom sustained the alliance with a revamped populism that combined progressive economic policy with hillbilly music and backwoods mannerisms.

If Folsom's stump tactics were conventional, his views on race relations were not. He had found blacks to be "good citizens," he said, "and if they had been making a living for me like they have for [whites in] the Black Belt, I'd be proud of them instead of kicking them and cussing them all the time." He openly supported the efforts of Alabama blacks to regain the right to vote, and he

"Big Jim" Folsom

appointed people who shared that view to positions where they could influence registration. He watched with amusement as the Alabama legislature, with all the subtlety, grace, and effect of "a hound dog baying at the moon," found ways to record its disapproval of integration. He vetoed legislative attempts to cripple the NAACP and intimidate its members, although the legislature predictably overrode most of those vetoes. When a bill passed permitting local officials to consider the general welfare of the community and several other superficially nonracial factors in assigning children to schools, Folsom let the measure become law without his signature. This pupil-placement law had so much legislative support that a veto would have served only a symbolic purpose anyway.

Folsom's failure to champion segregation was a sin of omission that he soon compounded. Adam Clayton Powell, the Harlem congressman who stood for everything the WCC abominated, visited Montgomery in November 1955 for a speech at Alabama State College. The governor had a cocktail with the visiting congressman—the alcohol alone disturbed many Southern Baptists—discussed the pace of Southern integration, and placed a limousine at

139

E. D. Nixon (left) and Adam Clayton Powell

Powell's disposal. Powell told his audience that Folsom had said integration was inevitable: "it is here now." The governor later protested that he had been misquoted, and that his reference had been to the nation, not to Alabama. He might have saved his effort, for he had bet on the wrong horse. Integration and black political participation would not come to Alabama soon enough to save Folsom's career. George Wallace, one of Folsom's ablest political lieutenants, carefully disassociated himself from the governor's increasingly unpopular views, a decision that indicated the force of the political gale. Three months after Powell's visit, Folsom admitted he "couldn't be elected dog-catcher." There were simply too few whites for whom segregation was personally inconvenient or morally offensive to sustain Folsom's moderation.[11]

BOYCOTT

Rosa Parks had had a hard day. As usual, she had fussed over fit and pinned and stitched hems at the Montgomery Fair, a department store where she worked. She had done a little shopping herself. The crowds were abnormally large with Christmas less than a month away, so Mrs. Parks hoped there would be a seat that evening on the bus that would take her home to Cleveland Avenue. She paid her fare and then stepped off to board in the rear, as local custom required. Because the rear section was full, she sat in one of the middle seats that blacks might occupy when whites did not.

The bus made slow progress around Court Square and stopped at the Empire Theater, where several white passengers boarded. In accordance with a municipal ordinance, the driver asked four blacks, including Mrs. Parks, to stand in order to seat the additional white passengers. Three blacks promptly complied. Mrs. Parks refused. "I don't really know why I wouldn't move," she said later.

> There was no plot or plan at all. I was just tired from shopping. I had my sacks and all, and my feet hurt.[12]

The driver found two policemen, who charged Mrs. Parks with violation of the city's segregation ordinance and ordered her to appear in court on Monday morning, December 5. Once booked, she called E. D. Nixon, for whom she had worked as a volunteer in the local office of the NAACP. Nixon spread the word.

Jo Ann Robinson reminded Nixon that plans to boycott the bus company had been shelved some months earlier. Both agreed that Mrs. Parks, who was well known and widely respected among Montgomery's blacks, presented an ideal symbol of the injustice of segregation. Dignified and diligent, forty-two years old, with coiled, braided hair and spectacles, Mrs. Parks was no pushy adolescent. After a momentary hesitation, Martin Luther King, Jr., volunteered his church for a planning session, to which Nixon and Mrs. Robinson invited leaders of the black community. Before the group could assemble, mimeographed leaflets proposing a boycott began to appear on the street.

The chance inquiry of an illiterate maid, unable to decipher one of those leaflets, alerted the *Montgomery Advertiser* to plans for a boycott. Or rather that was the explanation Joe Azbell used to protect his source, E. D. Nixon, who wanted a report in the Sunday paper to alert blacks who might not otherwise be informed. 141

Although Azbell knew Ralph Abernathy and had other contacts in the black community, his first story left some loose ends: he did not specify the "unidentified Negro leaders" who were organizing the protest; he knew that Rosa Parks' arrest was a critical event, but he had not interviewed her; he had no hint of the agenda for a "top secret" meeting scheduled for Monday evening at the Holt Street Baptist Church. Azbell did reach an official of Montgomery City Lines, who told him that the company and its drivers had "to obey laws just like any other citizen," as if that explained everything.[13]

Joe Azbell thought the city unnaturally quiet as he moved about on Monday. Even the throngs that surrounded the Holt Street Baptist Church seemed subdued when he arrived that evening. Inside, however, there was no hush, from the rousing initial chorus of "Onward Christian Soldiers" to the final shouted approval of a resolution to stay off the buses until the company agreed to hire black drivers, to guarantee courteous treatment of black passengers, and to permit first-come, first-served seating, whites from the front of the bus and blacks from the rear. Between the hymn and the

Addresses by King and other Montgomery pastors sustained enthusiasm for the boycott

business, speakers arrived and departed without introduction. One of them, an intense young man, reached for history to add significance to the moment: "And the history book will write of us as a race of people who in Montgomery County, State of Alabama, Country of the United States, stood up for and fought for their rights as American citizens, as citizens of democracy."

Martin Luther King, Jr., later remembered his peroration somewhat differently, but the exact words do not matter. Both the reporter and the unidentified (and to Azbell unknown) speaker sensed that the occasion was emotionally and historically important. King wanted to link moderation and militance in his speech, to inspire action and control it. He hoped his audience would extend their day-long boycott without becoming vindictive or violent. Azbell's account suggested that King had made his point:

> The meeting was much like an old-fashioned revival with loud applause added. It proved beyond any doubt there was a discipline among Negroes that many whites had doubted. It was almost a military discipline combined with emotion.[14]

Before

Montgomery's police commissioner thought the discipline came from systematic abuse by "Negro 'goon squads'" that kept nine of ten ordinary passengers off the buses. He assigned police to bus stops to prevent violence and ordered motorcycle policemen to convoy buses in the first days of the boycott. Ironically, this unusual protection may have increased participation, for some blacks apparently assumed they would be arrested for taking a bus.[15]

All those policemen made one arrest—a nineteen-year-old charged with preventing an elderly woman from riding a bus. A few days later, a judge threw the case out of court when the woman testified that the thoughtful young man had been assisting her through a busy intersection. The absence of evidence did not prevent whites from regularly attributing the boycott's success to intimidation. That explanation held blacks at fault, exonerated segregation, and suggested that only terror could achieve black unity. Black spokesmen responded that conscience, not force, sus-

After

tained the boycott. King later wrote that no wholly secular explanation would do; divine inspiration, he said, produced the dignified resistance of Montgomery's blacks. If not divine inspiration, Joe Azbell thought, at least forty-odd inspired preachers who presided at twice-weekly prayer meetings where audiences joyously rededicated themselves to the cause.[16]

The dedication of Montgomery blacks was almost universal. Prominent "big Negroes" drove their big cars to take maids and handymen to work in white neighborhoods. Black owners of taxicabs charged their patrons bus fare. Hundreds of blacks insisted on walking to make their participation completely visible. J. H. Bagley, the bus company's local manager, estimated that the boycott was 90 percent effective and that "thousands" of riders had stayed off the buses. The *Advertiser* printed a photograph showing a solitary black figure in front of benches where ordinarily, the caption read, "several hundred Negroes" would be waiting. Yet most blacks somehow

145

went where they wanted to go. Many attended the routine five-minute trial of Rosa Parks; she did not testify, was fined $10 and $4 costs, and filed a notice of appeal.

From the outset, the Montgomery Improvement Association (MIA), which represented boycotting blacks, offered to negotiate with the bus company and with the city. Jack Crenshaw, counsel for the bus line and the person who appears to have controlled the company's policy, may have misinterpreted that openness as a sign of weakness. The company held franchises from several Southern cities, and Crenshaw may have thought that any willing retreat from segregation would endanger every Southern contract. In any case, he apparently decided to do nothing without a court order. He would trade the permanent good will of Southern whites for the temporary loss of patronage by Montgomery's blacks. Until the threats and the violence ceased, Crenshaw said, the company would not even meet representatives of the MIA. (His reference to violence rested on reports by drivers of a few rocks thrown and fewer bullets fired at buses; Crenshaw assumed blacks were responsible.)[17]

Accompanied by Nixon, Rosa Parks arrives for her trial

Suspecting that positions would soon become rigid, the executive director of the Alabama Council on Human Relations invited representatives of the MIA to meet with the city commissioners and officials of the company. The parley did not go well. As president of the MIA, King deplored violence, offered to report to police any offenders the organization discovered, and restated the black community's terms for ending the boycott. Crenshaw replied that the company could not permit first-come, first-served seating without a change in the city's segregation ordinance. Police Commissioner Clyde Sellers and Mayor W. A. ("Tacky") Gayle wanted no part of that hot potato and seemed to King to become "more and more intransigent" after Crenshaw had argued that point. The company would not consider hiring black drivers, but Crenshaw promised that white drivers would in the future be more courteous. Martin Luther King, Jr., among others, had heard that before. He suggested that the fruitless discussion end.[18]

Apparently hoping a less charged atmosphere would have a better result, Mayor Gayle asked King and a few other MIA members to remain for informal conversation. Commissioner Frank A. Parks, an interior decorator at the beginning of his first term in public office, seemed ready to accept the MIA's seating proposal. "We can work it within our segregation laws," Parks said, indicating his agreement with a legal contention of the MIA. Crenshaw firmly contradicted him, and Parks soon backed down. Besides, Crenshaw went on, "If we granted the Negroes these demands, . . . they would go about boasting of a victory they had won over the white people; and this we will not stand for."[19]

That aside helps explain the inflexible response of white supremacists to the most trivial request for changed racial practice. Any concession made under pressure would indicate both white weakness and black strength, and thereby subvert racist mythology: white men could make no concession without endangering white women. Subsequent meetings discovered no way around the impasse and both sides prepared for a siege instead of a settlement.

Indeed the company began these preparations so promptly that they were probably intended to force the MIA to a settlement. On the second day of the boycott, the local manager linked reduced revenue and reduced service. On the third day, curtailment began. Before the week was out, service to most of the city's black neighborhoods had been suspended, a step that certainly assisted advocates of the boycott. The emotional pitch in the black community drooped as the week wore on. One drenched student at Alabama State College announced that his principles would not survive one more day of rain. But when the determination of the black community faltered, there were no buses to board.[20]

King and the MIA ran into official hostility as they improvised to provide other means of transportation. A letter from the city comptroller reminded owners of taxis that the standard fee schedule had the force of a municipal ordinance; he had heard, he continued, that some black operators were charging bus fare instead. The police chief reported "numerous complaints" about overloaded vehicles and ordered the force to be especially vigilant in checking car pools. As the weeks became months and the boycott drew national attention and support, the MIA set up regular assembly and dispatch points, raised money and purchased new station wagons, and hired full-time drivers. When somebody dumped acid on those shiny station wagons, the police were baffled.[21]

Although transportation became readily available, some blacks continued to walk. The protest was for them a spiritual odyssey and the hardship a price they willingly paid for equality. King used the remarks of several anonymous walking blacks to illustrate for national audiences the dignified faith with which blacks met white oppression. An older woman overcame her obvious fatigue and declined a ride from one of the MIA's drivers: "I'm not walking for myself," she explained. "I'm walking for my children and grandchildren." Another woman made the same point: "My feet is tired, but my soul is at rest."[22]

This resigned, Christian resistance to injustice was soon associated with the leadership of Martin Luther King, Jr., although his synthesis of ideology and tactic was neither original nor fully developed when the boycott commenced in December 1955. King brought no preconceived formula to events in Montgomery; indeed

148

he did some prayerful rationalization to differentiate the MIA's boycott from unjust economic coercion of the sort advocated by White Citizens' Councils. As the boycott progressed, King gradually fused elements of Christian idealism, Gandhian nonviolence, and civil disobedience into a creed that inspired others and gave him a moral assurance that compensated for youthful inexperience, temper, and doubt.

He had some help from a gentle, sheltered, white librarian, who wrote a remarkable letter to the *Montgomery Advertiser* a week after the boycott began. "Not since the first battle of the Marne has the taxi been put to as good use as it has been this past week in Montgomery," Juliette Morgan began. Yet the city's blacks, she thought, owed more to the example of Gandhi's Salt March and to

Boycott poster removed by city police from bus stops. The poster says: "Remember we are fighting for a cause. Do not ride a bus today."

Thoreau's work on civil disobedience than to the inspiration of French troops. Montgomery's blacks faced greater obstacles than had Gandhi, for Southern whites held their prejudices more tenaciously than Great Britain had held the empire. Yet "passive resistance combined with freedom from hate" might be sufficient to the task. She dismissed as absurd the moral equation of the bus boycott with the economic coercion of the WCC; compare the speeches of white supremacists with those Joe Azbell reported from the meeting at the Holt Street Church, she urged, "and blush."

Miss Morgan borrowed the ingratiating device of white supremacists who prefaced their prejudice with protests of affection for blacks. She had ridden Montgomery's buses for fourteen years, she wrote, and she named several considerate drivers. Others, by contrast, used "the tone and manners of mule drivers in their treatment of Negro passengers." Several times she had herself left buses in indignation at discourtesy toward black passengers. For years, they had paid "full fare for fourth class service," and Miss Morgan could

150

muster no sympathy for the economic plight of Montgomery City Lines. She summarized Crenshaw's argument as "Ye rebels! Disperse!" and punctured his pompous pretense of law and order. "I find it ironical," she wrote, "to hear men in authority ... speak piously of law enforcement" while they are "openly flouting" the Supreme Court's interpretation of the Constitution. The incidence of violence, about which municipal authorities pretended disquiet, was trivial in comparison to the riots that greeted the abolition of fraternities and sororities at Montgomery's Lanier High School.

The United States of America, Miss Morgan reminded Montgomery, had been "founded upon a boycott" of British tea. And now, she felt,

> history is being made in Montgomery. . . . It is hard to imagine a soul so dead, a heart so hard, a vision so blinded and provincial as not to be moved with admiration at the quiet dignity, discipline, and dedication with which the Negroes have conducted their boycott. . . . Their cause and their conduct have filled me with great sympathy, pride, humility, and envy. I envy their unity, their good humor, their fortitude, and their willingness to suffer for great Christian and democratic principles, or [for] just plain decent treatment.

"This may be a minority report," she concluded, "but a number of Montgomerians not entirely inconsequential agree with my point of view."[23]

Juliette Morgan may well have estimated accurately the support for integration among Montgomery's whites, but she overestimated their courage and perhaps even her own, for she became a pariah among whites and took her life in the summer of 1957. In the first days of the boycott, however, Juliette Morgan was not alone. Mrs. I. B. Rutledge had conducted an unscientific survey without finding "one white person who feels that it is right that a Negro be made to stand that a white person may sit." "Isn't it time," she asked, for "those of us who really believe in Christian and democratic principles ... to speak out and help create a public opinion" that will permit a compromise?

Several other letter writers—almost exclusively women—agreed that, as one woman wrote, "the treatment of Negroes in our city

151

buses has caused us to bow our heads in shame." Another had had enough of the defensive fantasy of white supremacists: "I am afraid," she wrote, "that the Negro is not now, nor has ever been, as happy and content with his place as we southern whites have believed." Grover Hall, the *Advertiser*'s editor, concurred. The white community, he said, had "kidded itself into believing" that terror explained the boycott and that "Negroes were happy in their state." Hall's initial editorial response suggested that first-come, first-served seating was not unthinkable, "if the grievance is confined to that."[24]

But many whites quickly decided, as Jack Crenshaw had, that the grievance was not confined to that. Whatever the MIA said, many whites apparently believed the demand reached beyond equal, if separate, seats on buses to integration everywhere. Crenshaw's fear of any concession crept through the white community, as Grover Hall later confirmed: "The whites ... are persuaded that they cannot allow themselves to be overcome on this terrain, ill-chosen ... though it is, lest they be routed in the schools." Hall himself had first commended the city's "admirable coolness," but he soon lost his. Perhaps he was unconscious of his military metaphor, but the mask of moderation slipped when he warned Negro leaders to "reckon with two realities."

> The white man's economic artillery is far better emplaced, and commanded by more experienced gunners.
>
> Second, the white man holds all the offices of government.... There will be white rule as far as the eye can see.... Does any Negro leader doubt that the resistance to ... Negro voting has ... increased?[25]

Hall held out the prospect of future suffrage (which the Fifteenth Amendment had guaranteed more than eighty years before) in response to a request for a seat on the bus. And he suggested that refusal of that unresponsive offer meant war.

But Hall did not blame black activism on Communists as other Southern whites sometimes did. Black unity in Montgomery, a correspondent of the *Advertiser* observed, derived from organization across the entire South, a circumstance that "must be a delight

to Communists everywhere." Hall scoffed at the notion that the
NAACP was a Communist front and assured his readers that racial
agitation would continue even if Alabama's politicians succeeded in
their effort to banish the NAACP. The editor asked one persistent
woman how she knew that Communists were managing the boycott. "It just stands to reason," was her earnest reply.[26]

It just stood to reason, from her perspective, because it was
happening all over the South. While Montgomery's blacks stayed off
the buses, other blacks in other places began to use public facilities.
In Tuscaloosa, a black graduate student enrolled at the University of
Alabama, where her brief appearance caused a riot, her suspension,
readmission, and expulsion—with more court appearances and large
headlines at each step. Almost every meeting of every state legislature and city council was preoccupied with the search for new
devices to protect segregation. Although state courts usually proved
reliable allies, federal courts did not, and informal enforcement
through custom and subtle intimidation began to break down.

In this atmosphere, as Jack Crenshaw had perceived at the outset of the boycott, any black request was an entering wedge, any white concession an acceptance of "race-mixing." A seat in the front of the bus would lead to "a seat at the white lunch counter and [to] colored sales girls." Whites might responsibly encourage blacks to raise their standard of living, so long as changes did "not lay the foundation for ultimate intermarriage [and] the disintegration of the white race." A boycott was "a strike against the white people to gain superiority." The MIA advertised both its limited objective and its willingness to negotiate. But whites did not take the organization at its word, and the continuing success of the boycott undoubtedly checked the readiness of black leaders to make concessions.[27]

In spite of stiffening resolve on both sides, Mayor Gayle at last found the elusive compromise. On Sunday, January 22, he announced that the city commission, the bus company, and a group of "prominent Negro ministers . . . representing the Negroes of Montgomery" had settled the dispute, and that bus service in the black neighborhoods would resume promptly. The negotiators had agreed, Gayle went on, that the company had complete authority to hire drivers and must obey applicable regulations requiring segregation. The company promised "uniform courtesy" to all patrons, and first-come, first-served seating in the middle section of the buses; whites would fill that section from the front, where ten seats were to be reserved, and blacks from the rear. Gayle had somehow induced black representatives to accept terms Jack Crenshaw would have offered weeks before and which blacks had subsequently rejected several times. It was a spectacular triumph.

But the mayor had made it up. The MIA disavowed the unidentified "prominent Negro ministers," who protested that they had been "hoodwinked," and whose version of the conference differed from the one Gayle gave the press. King and other members of the MIA visited taverns and other Saturday-night haunts to be sure that early reports did not deceive blacks who might not be in church on Sunday. By Monday morning, Gayle's settlement looked like a called bluff.[28]

154

And the mayor was angry. "We have pussyfooted around on this boycott long enough," Gayle told Joe Azbell. Apparently the city's blacks had become convinced "that they have the white people hemmed up in a corner," Gayle continued, and that they need not "give an inch until they force the white people . . . to submit to their demands—in fact to swallow all of them." The blacks were mistaken, the mayor said, for most whites did not "care whether a Negro ever rides a bus again," especially if that act endangered "the social fabric of our community." Make no mistake, Gayle repeated; the goal was nothing less than the "destruction of our social fabric." To save it, he said, he and Commissioner Parks had joined the White Citizens' Council, as Commissioner Sellers had done some weeks before. Martin Luther King, Jr., Grover Hall observed, had managed to make the WCC respectable; "the Southern Moderate," Hall continued, "is as nearly extinct as the whooping crane."

Certainly the white people of Montgomery appeared to approve Gayle's outburst and the city's new "get-tough" policy. The switchboard at city hall handled "hundreds of telephone calls praising the mayor and the commissioners." Commissioner Parks reported that "dozens" of businessmen would institute a counterboycott and fire their black employees. Commissioner Sellers instructed police to disperse groups waiting for car pools. Mayor Gayle loosed a tirade against timid whites who paid cab fare or otherwise subsidized the boycott and thereby encouraged black radicalism. "The Negroes have made their own bed," Gayle said, "and the whites should let them sleep in it."[29]

A plague of legal difficulties beset black leaders. Pending the outcome of cases the boycott had set in motion, Rosa Parks declined to pay her $10 fine; the judge offered her jail instead. Martin Luther King, Jr., spent a few anxious hours in the Montgomery jail on a charge of speeding. Four times insurers cancelled liability coverage for automobiles in the MIA's car pool. The local draft board abruptly revoked the occupational deferment of the young black attorney who had charted the MIA's course in the courts. Fred Gray was reclassified and available for immediate induction. His appeal moved like a yo-yo through the Selective Service hierarchy until officials in Washington reversed the Montgomery County board, an affront that triggered several resignations and a temporary refusal to provide any draftees from Alabama.

Of course somebody decided that legal harassment accomplished too little, too slowly. Martin Luther King, Jr., was preaching at one of the regular prayer meetings when the bomb thumped on the front porch of his house. Startled by the noise, Coretta Scott King moved toward their infant daughter, who was asleep at the rear of the residence. The bomb shattered the front window, tore a hole in the porch, and battered a column, but injured no one. By the time King reached the house, several hundred blacks had gathered in the area. The crowd's ugly mood frightened Joe Azbell, Mayor Gayle, Commissioner Sellers, and the white policemen who had rushed to the scene. "I was terrified," one officer recalled. "I owe my life to that nigger preacher, and so do all the other white people who were there."[30]

King could not resist pointing out the logical consequences of "get-tough" public statements when Sellers and Gayle privately deplored violence. But King had swallowed his resentment by the

On King's bomb-damaged porch. At King's right (in uniform), Mayor Gayle; Commissioner Sellers at King's left.

time all three men went out on the blasted porch to try to calm the crowd. As he began, the young minister must have been speaking as much to himself as to the black faces in the darkness:

> We believe in law and order. Don't get panicky. Don't do anything panicky at all. Don't get your weapons. He who lives by the sword shall perish by the sword. . . . We are not advocating violence. We want to love our enemies.

He shifted to the first person singular as he regained his confidence:

> I want you to love your enemies. Be good to them. . . . I did not start this boycott. I was asked by you to serve as your spokesman. I want it to be known the length and breadth of this land that if I am stopped this movement will not be stopped. For what we are doing is right. What we are doing is just. And God is with us.

King's touch with the crowd was perfect. Back came a chorus of "Amens" and "God bless yous" that turned to jeers when Gayle and Sellers promised an unstinting search for the bomber and protection for King and his family. King spoke the benediction:

> Go home and don't worry. Be calm as I and my family are. We are not hurt, and remember that if anything happens to me, there will be others to take my place.[31]

King's words did not end the sporadic violence; a few days later, a small bomb missed Nixon's house and smashed the fence in his yard. But both sides took steps to transfer the quarrel to the courts. On behalf of five black women, Fred Gray filed a suit in federal court asking that local and state regulations requiring segregated seating be declared unconstitutional. About the same time, a county grand jury, which included one black member, began weighing the prosecutor's evidence that the boycott was an illegal conspiracy against the bus company. No one could be compelled to patronize a business, Judge Eugene Carter explained to the jurors. On the other hand, "the right to conduct one's business without wrongful interference" was "a valuable property right" that merited legal protection. If the jurors found the boycott illegal, they could indict the leaders. On February 21, 1956, the second day of Brotherhood Week, the grand jury identified and indicted 115 leaders. It was, Grover Hall said later, "the dumbest act that was ever done in Montgomery."[32]

The grand jury's list, which contained some duplications and several unaccountable omissions, lamented the "exemplary race relations" the boycott had impaired. The jurors exhorted "leaders of both races"—including presumably most of those under indictment—"to take a long and thoughtful look into the future." The grand jury then looked itself and saw no end to segregation:

> In this state we are committed to segregation by custom and by law; we intend to maintain it. The settlement of differences over school attendance, public transportation and other public facilities must be made within these laws which reflect our way of life.[33]

Bombs and indictments indicated the "growing tension" and spreading "hate" that the grand jury noted during the third month of the boycott. Reverend Thomas Thrasher, one of the white clergymen on the Alabama Council on Human Relations, wrote of the "universal . . . fear" that gripped the community:

> The businessman's fear lest his business be destroyed by some false move or baseless rumor. The Negro's fear for his safety and his job. The clergy's fear that their congregations may be divided. . . . The politician's fear that he may do something disapproved by a majority of voters. And finally the whole community's fear that we may be torn asunder by a single rash act precipitating racial violence.[34]

It did not matter, Joe Azbell asserted, who caused the violence. What did matter was that

> bombs are being tossed in a good city where good people live. What does matter is that none of this racial strife, this bomb throwing, and this harsh bickering is adding to the solution of the community's ticklish racial problem. It is adding to the problem.

Azbell doubted that more argument would change minds or leave a legacy of brotherhood. "All of us," he urged, must "tone down our feelings" lest a "full-scale racial war" sweep Montgomery. Blacks could reduce that danger immediately, he suggested, by ending their

Hostile stares for King and Abernathy

boycott. Tactical retreat would cost almost nothing, since they would surely win the court case that would require whites to make the final concessions. In fact, King may have considered the course Azbell recommended, but it did not gain wide acceptance and the moment passed.[35]

Conciliators made no headway because both sides had handed the dispute to the courts. Conviction of the boycott's hundred-odd leaders, whites believed, would end the social pressure that kept blacks off the buses. Blacks, on the other hand, confident that their suit doomed segregated buses in Montgomery, turned the arrest of their leaders into a holiday. Sheriff's deputies brought in and booked Ralph Abernathy and others whose names headed the list. As word spread, blacks stopped at the station to find out if they were included; those omitted seemed more downcast than those indicted. Corridors filled with joking blacks, who helped the deputies with unfamiliar names and addresses. The atmosphere, Joe Azbell wrote, was "much like 'old home week.'" Martin Luther King, Jr., was out of town and could not surrender until the following day.

King was the first defendant called a month later to the drab courtroom where Judge Carter heard the case without a jury. The state had little difficulty demonstrating that there was a boycott and that King had had a good deal to do with it. Intimidation and violence, the prosecution contended, meant that the conspirators had not merely, and legally, withheld their patronage, but had violated the law. Two witnesses testified that their refusal to observe the boycott had led to harassment and harm; the state might have selected more credible witnesses, however, than an employee of the county and the maid who worked for Mayor Gayle's mother-in-law. To connect King to the violence during the boycott, the prosecutor asked Joe Azbell if King's speeches had been inflammatory. No, Azbell replied, undermining the state's case; King had consistently counseled nonviolence.

In spite of his own anticlimactic testimony, Azbell thought the prosecution had made a reasonable presentation. King's defense rested on his contention that the boycott (if there was a boycott, which his lawyers did not concede) had "just cause" within the meaning of the Alabama statute. This contention permitted King's

Crowd awaits verdict in King's trial

Guilty!

lawyers to call witness after witness who told of degrading discourtesy and physical mistreatment at the hands of callous drivers. King's own testimony was not heroic, but convenient lapses of memory did not prevent his conviction. Judge Carter offered King a choice of a fine of $500 or 386 days at hard labor. The penalty was low, Carter said, because King had earnestly tried to keep the protest peaceful. Unmoved by the judge's compassion, King posted bond and appealed.[36]

The arrests and the trial put the boycott on the front page of the *New York Times* and the editorial page of the *Washington Post*, brought a *Life* photographer to Montgomery, and stimulated requests for presidential intervention from Adam Clayton Powell and the bishops of the African Methodist Episcopal Church. While the trial was in progress, a reporter asked for Eisenhower's reaction. Well, the President replied, he was not much of a lawyer. The rest of his answer was vintage Eisenhowerese, both in style and in content:

> I do believe that it is incumbent on all the South to show some progress. . . . I believe we should not stagnate, but again I plead for understanding, for really sympathetic consideration of a problem that is far larger, both in its emotional and even in its physical aspects than most of us realize.

161

The President summarized: "As far as I am concerned, I am for moderation, but I am for progress; that is exactly what I am for in this thing."[37]

However fuzzy, the President was entitled to his opinion. But Joe Azbell and Grover Hall wearied of the opinions of out-of-town journalists who visited Montgomery briefly and filed stories based more on preconception than investigation. The Montgomery Azbell and Hall knew was not benighted, and they bristled when simplistic self-righteousness passed for journalism. They began interviewing their professional guests about race relations where they came from. The resulting articles sounded like the pot calling the kettle names, but the *Advertiser*'s point that prejudice was no local phenomenon deserved a hearing.

By the spring of 1956, the boycott was no local phenomenon either. White supremacists, arguing that compromise in Montgomery would bring race-mixing elsewhere, enlisted national assistance. Those of both races who favored integration provided the financial and legal support that kept the MIA's station wagons on the streets and its lawyers in the courts. Local leaders—especially Martin Luther King, Jr.—had made out-of-town promises and had built national constituencies that had to be satisfied. The case pending in the federal courts effectively removed legal issues from local control, even if local leaders had been able to arrange a settlement. There was not much to do but wait.

Municipal officials did pull one last string. They alleged that the MIA's car pool was an unlicensed form of public transportation and went back to Judge Carter for an injunction. Martin Luther King, Jr., wondered why they had waited so long. The proceeding did not require a legal defense of segregation and would be difficult for the MIA to appeal to the federal courts. And an injunction, which King expected, might undermine the morale of the black community to the point that the boycott could not be sustained. Those polished station wagons were rolling symbols of success, a constant source of pride to blacks and of irritation for white supremacists. Even blacks who chose to walk drew inspiration and comfort from the knowledge that they could ride if they wished.

So King was apprehensive as he returned to Judge Carter's courtroom in mid-November 1956. He heard attorneys outline the city's case and then, in an entirely different mood, watched the charade play out to the injunction he had once feared. For by the time Judge Carter issued his ruling, it was irrelevant; as proceedings began in Montgomery, the Supreme Court of the United States ruled that ordinances requiring segregated seating violated the Fourteenth Amendment. The MIA could abandon the car pool and comply with Carter's injunction because Montgomery City Lines had to abandon segregation and comply with the order of the Supreme Court. The decision seemed almost providential: "God Almighty has spoken from Washington, D.C.," remarked a spectator in the Montgomery courthouse.[38]

It took nearly a month for the official word to reach Montgomery. In the interim, a solemn march of the Ku Klux Klan roused derision rather than terror among Montgomery's newly confident blacks,

and the city commissioners did nothing to prepare the community for the "tremendous impact" they warned that the decision would have. Instead they clung to their get-tough policy:

> The City Commission, and we know our people are with us in this determination, will not yield one inch, but will do all in its power to oppose the integration of the Negro race with the white race in Montgomery, and will forever stand like a rock against social equality, intermarriage, and mixing of the races under God's creation and plan.

King and the MIA used the interval to instruct blacks in courtesy that bordered on deference and in nonviolent response to provocation. On the morning of December 21, as he had done more than a year earlier, King got up to meet the first bus of the day. With Nixon, Abernathy, and a host of journalists and photographers, he waited for the vehicle to pull to the curb. "I believe you are the Reverend King, aren't you?" the driver asked. "We are glad to have you this morning." Later that day, a disgruntled rider looked around another bus and remarked emphatically, "I see this isn't going to be a white Christmas." One of the black passengers replied gently, "Yes, sir, that's right." "Suddenly, astonishingly," a reporter noted, "everybody on the bus was smiling."[39]

There were, of course, sullen people on other buses. And there were shots, one of which hit a black passenger in the leg, and bombs, which damaged the homes and churches of several clergymen identified with the boycott, including Abernathy. A grand jury indicted seven white men for the bombings, but the two brought to trial were not convicted. Charges against the other five, and the still-pending indictments of black leaders for violating the antiboycott law, were dropped simultaneously. When legal technicalities jeopardized his appeal, King quietly paid his $500 fine. The cases were closed, the boycott concluded.

CHRISTIANITY AND COMMUNITY

In spite of tension, temper, get-tough statements, bigotry, and bombs, no one had been killed. In part, Montgomery's good fortune was simply good fortune: dynamite and bullets and boycott-connected automobile accidents might have been fatal. More important than luck, however, was the strategy Montgomery's blacks had adopted. Unlike the sit-ins, protest marches, and demonstrations that came later in the civil rights crusade, a boycott kept the races apart and prevented the confrontation that led to violence. Furthermore, Montgomery in 1955 was no anonymous metropolis. If there was less interracial contact than white people thought, at least white people knew one another, had attended school together, belonged to the same clubs, read the same newspapers. Civic leaders had roots in the region, contact with their constituents, and pride in the city's growth. When the *Advertiser* or a group of business leaders preached patience and peace, people listened, and most of them heeded.

That same sense of community among blacks made the boycott effective and suppressed potential violence. In particular, black pastors knew one another and effectively led their congregations. Christian nonviolence was a familiar concept, spiritually nourishing as well as tactically promising, partly because many whites were earnest Christians too. Although Montgomery's churches were racially separate and differed on doctrinal details, the whole community at least outwardly respected Christian teaching. A great many had an inner commitment as well.

That Christian commitment was not so universal as it had once been in the United States. Secularization had gradually diminished the moral force of Christianity among both blacks and whites. Martin Luther King, Jr., would have to learn, a skeptic remarked, that the world was not just one big Baptist church, and that Christian nonviolence would not open every heart and every door. Neither Christianity nor nonviolence, for instance, inspired Northern ghettoes, where Muslims and other militants would in the coming decade counter King's ideas with black separatism. And the NAACP, the institutional expression of black aspirations for more than a generation, relied more heavily on the Constitution and the courts than on Christianity.

The leaders of the NAACP recognized King's charisma and acknowledged the tactical usefulness of nonviolence. But the

165

NAACP had pointedly not endorsed the boycott at the outset, partly because an endorsement might have undermined the MIA's reiterated contention that the boycott was a local movement with specific objectives, and partly because those objectives, in the view of the NAACP, were too limited. Only when the boycott reached the courts, where for the first time the MIA broadened its challenge to segregation as a system, did the NAACP offer assistance. King's methods, leaders of the NAACP held, derived more from local circumstance than some of his enthusiastic followers recognized. Nonviolence and passive resistance did in fact attract the spotlight of national publicity and aroused the nation's liberal sympathy. But the media and liberal sentiment, however important, contributed less to the success of the boycott, the NAACP argued, than court orders and economic power.[40] The loss of three-quarters of its revenue captured the attention of Montgomery City Lines in a way no ideology could. And the city fathers found a court order more compelling than conscience.

Rosa Parks in the front of the bus

That view of events did not hold that King was mistaken, but only that his methods were not universally applicable and were not in themselves sufficient to achieve racial justice. The Southern Christian Leadership Conference (SCLC), which became his organizational expression in the years after Montgomery, did not directly integrate many schools, register many black voters, or modify economic institutions that discriminated on the basis of race. Indeed the SCLC sometimes seemed an organization in search of a cause, although King himself was perpetually leading a march or a demonstration. Because of the errors of whites, or the economic and political leverage of blacks, or the legal result of local circumstance, or the persuasive power of Christian nonviolence, some of those demonstrations accomplished their purpose. And win or lose, in a sense, King accomplished his purpose. For if he never narrowed his effort to one objective, he did focus on principles. And his statement of those principles lifted the aspirations of millions of Americans of both races and helped make the nation's racial practice slightly more congruent with its equalitarian ideal.

Notes

[1] George Barrett, "Jim Crow, He's Real Tired," in *New York Times Magazine*, March 3, 1957, p. 11.

[2] George Barrett, "Montgomery: Testing Ground," in *New York Times Magazine*, December 16, 1956, p. 48.

[3] *Montgomery Advertiser*, December 17, 22, 1955; see also Jim Bishop, *The Days of Martin Luther King, Jr.* (New York: G. P. Putnam's Sons, 1971), p. 175.

[4] Martin Luther King, Jr., *Stride Toward Freedom* (New York: Harper & Row, 1958), chapter 2.

[5] Thomas R. Thrasher, "Alabama's Bus Boycott," in *The Reporter*, March 8, 1956, p. 16.

[6] *Montgomery Advertiser*, July 20, 1955.

[7] *Ibid.*, August 25, 1955.

[8] *Ibid.*, July 15, 24, 1955.

[9] *Ibid.*, October 11, 1955; see also *ibid.*, October 3–7, 1955.

[10] *Ibid.*, February 22, 1956.

[11] *Ibid.*, July 7, 1955; August 12, 1955; September 18, 1955; October 4, 1955; November 4, 5, 1955; January 26, 1956; March 4, 1956; see also *New York Times*, February 25, 1956.

[12] *Time*, January 3, 1964, pp. 14–15; Interview with Joe Azbell, November 27, 1975.

[13] *Montgomery Advertiser*, December 4, 1955; Azbell interview.

[14] *Montgomery Advertiser*, December 7, 1955.

[15] *Ibid.*, December 4, 5, 1955; January 17, 1956; see also Norman E. Walton, "The Walking City: A History of the Montgomery Boycott," in *Negro History Bulletin*, October 1956, p. 18.

[16] *Montgomery Advertiser*, December 6, 8, 1955; King, *Stride*, p. 69; Azbell interview, December 13, 1975.

[17] *Montgomery Advertiser*, December 6–8, 1955.

[18] *Ibid.*, December 9, 13, 1955; King, *Stride*, pp. 109–112.

[19] King, *Stride*, p. 112.

[20] Walton, "Walking City," p. 18.

[21] Walton, "Walking City," in *Negro History Bulletin*, February, 1957, p. 104; *Montgomery Advertiser*, December 15, 16, 1955; King, *Stride*, p. 75ff.

[22] King, *Stride*, pp. 78, 10.

[23] *Montgomery Advertiser*, December 12, 1955.

[24] *Ibid.*, December 8, 9, 25, 1955; *U.S. News and World Report*, August 3, 1956, p. 84.

[25] *Montgomery Advertiser*, December 13, 1955; *U.S. News and World Report*, August 3, 1956, p. 86.

[26] *Montgomery Advertiser*, December 15, 22, 28, 1955; *U.S. News and World Report*, August 3, 1956, p. 84.

[27] *Montgomery Advertiser*, December 25, 1955; letters to the editor, January 2, 5, 8, 1956.

[28] *Ibid.*, January 22, 1956; King, *Stride*, pp. 124–26.

[29] *Montgomery Advertiser*, January 24, 25, 1956; *U.S. News and World Report*, August 3, 1956, p. 85.

[30] *Time*, February 18, 1957, p. 19.

[31] *Montgomery Advertiser*, January 31, 1956.

[32] *U.S. News and World Report*, August 3, 1956, p. 84.

[33] *Montgomery Advertiser*, February 22, 1956.

[34] Thrasher, "Boycott," p. 16.

[35] *Montgomery Advertiser*, February 6, 8, 1956.

[36] *Ibid.*, March 20–23, 1956.

[37] *Ibid.*, March 22, 1956.

[38] King, *Stride*, p. 160.

[39] *Ibid.*, pp. 170, 173; *Time*, December 31, 1956, p. 10.

[40] See, for example, the report of the NAACP convention in *New Republic*, July 16, 1956, pp. 9–10.

The Fuse Blows: 5
Watts, 1965

The 1960s began in hope and ended in shambles. Began with economic growth and ended with uncontrolled inflation. Began with the crooning of "We Shall Overcome" and ended with the shouting of "Black Power." Began with national consensus about a form of peace called "Cold War" and ended in division about a form of war called "pacification." Began in Camelot and ended in San Clemente, after disillusioning stops in Dallas and Memphis and several places in Vietnam.

There was no single turning point, no one decisive moment when the dream dissolved into nightmare. But an important moment occurred on the sultry evening of Wednesday, August 11, 1965, when Lee Minikus, an officer of the California Highway Patrol, turned on his siren and pursued a ten-year-old Buick up Los Angeles' Avalon Boulevard. The Buick eventually stopped, and Officer Minikus bantered with Marquette Frye, the young black driver. Minikus asked Frye for his license, which he had misplaced some time before. Minikus told Frye to walk a straight line and touch his nose with his finger; Frye failed both tests, and the two men joked about drinking. Attracted by the siren, a crowd collected and watched the good-natured interchange. Frye's stepbrother Ronald climbed out of the car to hear what was going on and "laugh a little bit myself."

Somebody moved off through a courtyard and across an alley to inform Frye's parents, who owned the car, of the arrest. Rena Frye, wearing a loose shift against the heat, interrupted the preparation of dinner and went to see for herself. She persuaded the police not to tow her car away, as was standard procedure in cases of drunken driving. Something she said to her son, or perhaps simply her presence, ended his good humor. In a flood of profanity, he announced that he would not go to the police station, a decision that Minikus and two other officers at the scene could not accept. One thing led to another, nightsticks to bruises, and Marquette, Ronald, and Rena Frye were handcuffed, shoved into a police car, and taken off to be booked. (Since Mrs. Frye was no longer available to move the car, it was towed off to storage; by the time she had located the vehicle at the end of a string of red tape, cumulative storage charges exceeded the car's value.)

The mood of the crowd soured with that of the central characters. Laughter turned to jeers and outrage matured from what had begun as a diverting incident. Catcalls and curses showed the abiding resentment of urban blacks for white policemen. Radios summoned more policemen and sirens more spectators to find out what was going on. Rumors circulated at the edge of the crowd and were carried to other crowds on other streets. Mrs. Frye's loose garb caused the most explosive one: white cops, the story ran, had manhandled a pregnant black woman. By the time the police withdrew with their prisoners, the spectators were ready to become participants. Somebody spat on one of the policemen, and two officers dragged Joyce Ann Gaines from the crowd. She was twenty years old and wearing the smock of her barber's trade. Rumor now made it two pregnant black women, and rocks, bricks, and bottles accompanied the last police cars to leave the intersection, a few blocks from the Los Angeles subdivision called Watts. A sweaty young black man in the midst of the crowd kept chanting "Burn, baby, burn."[1]

Only a few cars burned that first night. But before the week ended many other things lay in ashes. In a prophetic book published in 1963, the black novelist James Baldwin had reminded Americans of

Jeering the police

the ancient "rainbow sign": "No more water, the fire next time."
"The Negroes of this country," Baldwin warned, "may never be able
to rise to power, but they are very well placed indeed to precipitate
chaos and ring down the curtain on the American dream."[2]

They were well placed in the nation's cities where a transforma-
tion of urban life coincided with the influx of black residents and
the departure of many whites for the suburbs. Once a magnet for
ambitious Americans of every race, in the 1960s, the city became
instead a focus for many of the country's most vexing problems and
for much of the tension in American life. Urban expenditures for
welfare showed the economy's failure equitably to distribute prosperity. Any municipal court betrayed the breakdown of an ethic
that, more effectively than policemen, had once upheld law and
order. Transit, schools, and sanitation deteriorated, and riders, students, and the ordinary resident were badly served. Trapped industrial wastes and automotive exhausts made breathing unhealthy in

Burn, Baby, Burn

several American cities. Most obviously, these conditions prevailed in the black neighborhoods, the crowded ghettoes whose very existence challenged the nation's folklore about equality and opportunity and progress.

Even in California, which was popularly supposed to be the exception to most of the rules. One resident of Watts remembered his course to the golden land:

> We been to Mississippi and we been to Chicago. We been to New Orleans and we been to New York. And everywhere they say "Go to California!" California's the great big pot o' gold at the end of the rainbow. Well, now we're here in California, and there ain't no place else to go.[3]

No longer the land of infinite possibility, California was just the place where the continent ended and the dream ran out.

Watts did not look the way whites thought ghettoes ought to look: most of the dwellings along the broad streets in 1965 were single-family houses or duplexes, with attached garages, television antennae, and other evidence of an ability to consume. But appearance did not mislead the commission Governor Edmund G. ("Pat") Brown appointed to investigate the riots. The commission discovered a "dull, devastating spiral of failure" awaiting "the average disadvantaged child in the urban core." The commissioners outlined the dreary lives they foresaw for these children:

> His home life all too often fails to give him the incentive and the elementary experience with words and ideas which prepares most children for school. Unprepared and unready, he may not learn to read or write at all; and because he shares his problem with 30 or more in the same classroom, even the efforts of the most dedicated teachers are unavailing.

The "frustrated and disillusioned" student drops out and

> slips into the ranks of the permanent jobless, illiterate and untrained, unemployed and unemployable. . . . A family whose breadwinner is chronically out of work is almost invariably a disintegrating family. Crime rates soar and welfare rolls increase, even faster than the population.[4]

The commission's report described ghetto conditions that would become increasingly well known as the decade wore on: crowded classrooms, chronic unemployment, constant friction with police. Demographic data illustrated the pressure on black families, and the riots demonstrated why the public ought to be concerned. Three-quarters of the juveniles arrested during the riots came from broken homes. More than half of the heads of those families had no steady job; the family's income, much of which came from California's comparatively generous budget for public assistance, averaged about $300 per month. Nine of ten black families on the welfare rolls had no resident adult male; seven out of ten included at least one illegitimate child. Every census disclosed the explosive growth of this population. While the number of residents in the county had increased 13 percent, the budget for aid to dependent children had jumped 73 percent. In 1965, one in nine Americans was black, but the ratio dropped to one in seven under age fourteen and to one in six births. The median age of the white population was slightly over twenty-nine years. The median age of blacks was just over twenty-one; the median age in Watts was sixteen.[5]

"RIOTS WAITING TO HAPPEN"

The nation's political leaders, including President Lyndon B. Johnson, knew of conditions for which the phrase "urban crisis" became conventional political shorthand. Quite naturally, Johnson, "Pat" Brown, and their political allies publicly stressed legislation already passed, rather than instances of deprivation and discrimination that still plagued American society. The President, for instance, proudly and properly noted that he had had a hand in every civil rights law enacted since the days of Reconstruction. He promised a more equitable distribution of the nation's wealth after Congress enacted his "war on poverty" in 1964. Governor Brown remarked that a black in California could vote without hindrance and had "an equal right to any job for which he can qualify." "We have established these things in California," he asserted. The dimensions of public assistance in Los Angeles during the prosperous 1960s made Frank Murphy's program in depressed Detroit look like a nickel-and-dime operation. Murphy had wheedled about $20 million to help perhaps 200,000 people in 1931. By comparison, Los Angeles County routinely dispensed about $500 million to more than 300,000 people early in the 1960s.

Los Angeles, indeed, was a showplace for governmental programs. Welfare benefits, per-pupil expenditure for education, and unemployment compensation were generous. Antidiscrimination machinery was in place. County hospitals provided out-patient medical service. Virtually every federal agency showered money on the area. But instead of producing satisfaction, those actions may have aroused expectations that life in Watts could not satisfy. By creating and then dashing hope, some governmental measures may have heightened the anger of the people they were supposed to help.

So Los Angeles and several other American cities, as Senator Robert F. Kennedy later remarked, were "riots waiting to happen."

In fact urban America was, in a sense, chaos waiting to be discovered: the old institutions, designed for fewer people and simpler times, puffed on out of bureaucratic inertia, not because they worked. The collapse was as near as the closest school or bus stop, as evident as the smog overhead or the trash underfoot, as predictable as rising taxes and a rising rate of crime.

Few cities had adequate governmental resources for the tasks at hand. Los Angeles, for instance, was an advanced jurisdictional mess because literally dozens of municipal governments overlapped the authority of Los Angeles County. In addition, both state and nation relied on local agencies for the administration of other programs. Thus, as Paul Jacobs discovered,

> the county is responsible for welfare programs, the city for the school system; the county for health programs and air-pollution control, the city for police and garbage collections. . . . Primary taxing authority is vested in the county, but the city government controls the spending of some of the tax funds.[6]

How was anyone supposed to keep that straight? In particular, how was anyone who had not grown up in the area, or did not speak English or read well, or had to rely on public transportation, supposed to meet public obligations and receive public services? How were the poorer residents of Los Angeles—Spanish-speaking, black, yellow, or white—supposed to find the proper clerks to report the misconduct of a policeman, or the theft of a welfare check, or the loss of a son to the streets?

Still the public somehow struggled through the bureaucratic maze in numbers sufficient to overload public services. Teachers had too many students. Social workers had too many cases to consider carefully individual needs. Policemen had too many crimes to solve and too much traffic to control. Bus drivers had to charge too much and their patrons had to put up with too much inconvenience: in 1965, parts of Los Angeles simply could not be reached by 8:00 A.M., no matter what time one started at a bus stop in Watts.

Liberals usually argued that more governmental programs, and particularly more governmental dollars, could meet these urban

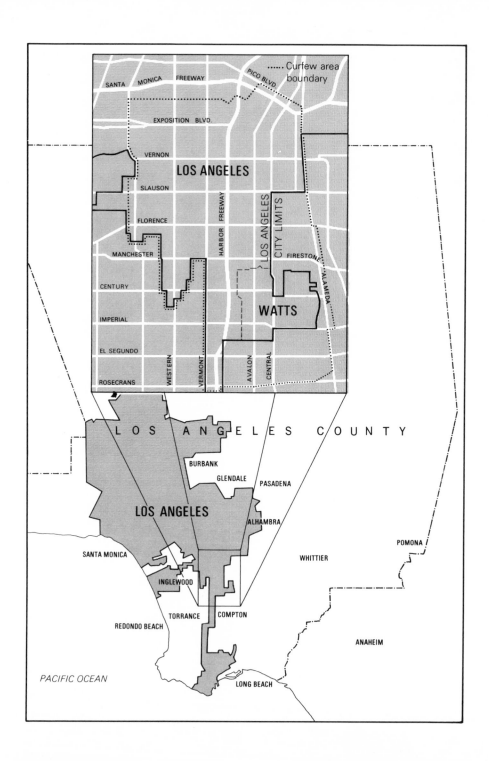

needs. But antidiscrimination programs already on statute books could not always be effectively enforced, and local taxpayers grew increasingly skeptical of increased expenditures for welfare. For many whites, the movement for civil rights ended when legislation in 1964 and 1965 opened public accommodations to black patrons and ballot boxes to black voters. Several proposals to escalate the war on poverty and to change programs for public assistance never received the requisite public or congressional support.

There was even some sentiment for reversing course. In its mildest guise, this white backlash had a tone of "what more do they want?" In its coarsest form, the backlash held that poverty derived from indolence and self-indulgence, and that government had unreasonably restricted the liberty of whites in an effort to prevent prejudice against blacks. This backlash was not exclusively a blue-collar phenomenon, although it certainly signalled the disenchantment of many white working people with elements of the urban liberal program. Whose jobs, they asked, did upwardly mobile blacks take, and whose unions did they join? Whose children attended the urban schools at the end of the bus line from the ghetto? Whose neighborhoods were on the fringe of black settlement, and whose property values were endangered? Why should ordinary people alone face the consequences of social experiments whose proponents shielded themselves with money and suburban boundaries?

The backlash was not exclusively white. Ten years of civil rights agitation had scarcely touched Northern ghettos; Martin Luther King, Jr., admitted in 1965 that his work had had little impact on blacks outside the South.[7] Black Muslims, on the other hand, a group with a growing following in Northern ghettos, did not share the hopes for integration held by King and Northern liberals. Founded in Detroit's Paradise Valley in the 1930s, Muslims advocated black pride and black power through the development of autonomous institutions, such as businesses, schools, and churches. Somewhat unfairly, militant blacks charged that a decade of politics and patience had not changed life for the ordinary ghetto black. Black power, some of these militants knew, included the power to take Northern cities apart.

177

"WE ARE ALL VICTIMS ..."

On the morning of Friday, August 13, 1965, thirty-six hours after Marquette Frye's arrest had set off two nights of rioting, Mayor Sam Yorty and Chief William Parker of the Los Angeles Police Department sent for more muscle. Because Governor Brown was vacationing in Greece, their request for help from the national guard went to Lieutenant Governor Glenn M. Anderson, who occupied a political hot seat. Anderson had to act for Governor Brown, who might second-guess any decision, and on the request of Mayor Yorty, who was a political rival of Brown and perhaps of Anderson himself. He was asked to send the overwhelmingly white national guard on a peacekeeping mission in an overwhelmingly black area, a situation with evident political risks. The investigative commission Brown later appointed, which distributed rebuke sparingly, thought Anderson "hesitated when he should have acted."[8] It was more than ten hours after Chief Parker's telephone call before the first guardsmen were available in Los Angeles, and more than twelve hours before they began to take up their posts around the city.

Lt. Gov. Glenn M. Anderson

Mayor Sam Yorty

It was not duty for which the guardsmen were well prepared. They had too much firepower, not enough training in crowd control, and almost no orientation from police. Many of the guardsmen knew little of Los Angeles and nothing at all of Watts. They could have used somewhat more detailed instructions as they set up and maintained their roadblocks. ("Turn left or get shot," was the way one outpost relayed its orders to startled motorists.) They had seen frightening headlines and televised pictures of rampaging mobs and roaring flames. Rumor had it that black snipers and terrorists, perhaps directed by the Vietcong, had organized to pick off patrolling guardsmen.[9] (The rumor was false, but the reference to the Vietcong was still appropriate, for domestic violence later in the decade was linked to mounting violence in Vietnam.) Yet, in spite of their inexperience and occasional lack of nerve, California's part-time soldiers finished their tour without making some of the errors their counterparts elsewhere on similar missions made later in the decade.

But people did get killed; Charles Patrick Fizer, for instance. Born in Louisiana, Fizer had grown up in Watts, singing in the choir of the Sweet Home Baptist Church, hanging on at school until the eleventh grade, catching a stray bullet while watching a gang fight, smoking marijuana, and being arrested. At fifteen, Fizer had begun to work as a nightclub singer; his most successful recording sold nearly a million copies. But without a second big hit, his career drifted. He was arrested for possession of barbiturates early in 1965 and released from custody on August 12.

The riots notwithstanding, Fizer immediately found a job as a busboy and worked through the night shift on Friday. When the restaurant did not open on Saturday, he borrowed a car, promising to return before the eight o'clock curfew that evening. But it was after nine when he paused some distance from a national guard roadblock. Ignoring the shouts and warning shots of the guardsmen, he suddenly accelerated toward the barricade. A guardsman fired at the car, which bounced off a building and stopped. Fizer was dead, a bullet in his brain, the twenty-third person to die during the riots.[10]

About thirty hours later, at four o'clock Monday morning, Joe Maiman, a balding Jewish milkman, drove his red Corvair into the forty-six-square-mile "curfew area" on his way to work. If he thought about the curfew, he probably did not think long, for he had driven those streets for years, including two trips after the curfew was established. He had the radio on, loudly, because he was rather hard of hearing, and he may not have heard the jeep pull up beside him in the intersection. A corporal, carrying a rifle, shouted "halt!"—an instruction Maiman may not have heard either—and approached the milkman's car. Startled, Maiman swung his vehicle toward the guardsman, who scrambled aboard the jeep and set off in pursuit. A second jeep, with a mounted machine gun, joined the chase. Two blocks from the intersection, the Corvair jumped the curb and stopped in the middle of a lawn. The machine gun had shattered the vehicle's back window and Joe Maiman's skull. He was the thirty-third, and, by the count of the governor's commissioners, the next-to-last to die.

Why did this pleasant, dependable, law-abiding man take off when a soldier asked him to stop? Maiman's brother answered the question with another in a letter to Governor Brown.

> How was my brother to have known whether those men who were chasing him were bona fide soldiers or hoodlums? I know if someone started shooting at me at 4 o'clock in the A.M. on a dark and lonely road during a period of rioting when lawlessness reigned supreme, I would have run just as fast as I could. You probably would have done the same. . . . I know it is too late to do anything about this. I am not bitter against the police, the National Guard or anyone else. We are all victims of a lawless age. Now there is nothing left except to attend his funeral and listen to the condolences from all who knew him.[11]

It was, of course, a "justifiable homicide," as was Charles Fizer's and each of twenty-four other deaths caused by law-enforcement officers. Some were more difficult to justify than Maiman's and Fizer's. Most were blacks who were arguably engaged in looting or identified—usually mistakenly—as snipers. The coroner's jury did not linger long. The one case of homicide that reached trial—against a black defendant who had allegedly caused the death of a white deputy sheriff—resulted in acquittal. About 350 people were convicted of felonies—chiefly theft—and about 1500 of misdemeanors.

Roadblock

Marquette Frye, whose arrest had started it all, and his brother Ronald pleaded guilty; their mother's conviction for interfering with a policeman was reversed on appeal.[12]

After their release on bail, all three Fryes had gone home and watched the riots on television. The next afternoon, Mrs. Frye attended a meeting called by blacks seeking to halt the disorders. "I am the woman who was arrested last night," she told the tense assembly. "I'm here to ask you please, to help me and to help others in this community to calm the situation down so that we will not have a riot tonight!"[13] Three days later, Marquette Frye took a different message to the Sunday congregation at the Muslim mosque. Just what he said is not completely clear, but there was no ambiguity about what he meant: he subscribed to the Muslim doctrine of black unity, and he had a developed antipathy for whites.

Marquette Frye had come a long way from the white friends of his integrated boyhood in Wyoming. When he had first arrived in Los

Rena and Marquette Frye

Angeles, his black contemporaries thought he "talked funny" and kept him at arm's length until he had learned to snatch purses and mastered other urban ways. Before the riots he had attended only one service at the Muslim mosque, partly because he knew of the Muslims' trouble with policemen. An incident at the mosque in 1962 had resulted in the death of one black and injury to six others, and was central to the conviction among blacks in Los Angeles that the police were prejudiced and brutal.

Chief Parker—a tough, tactless, professional cop—denied the charge. Strictly speaking, Parker was no bigot, an assistant attorney general of California once observed: the chief did not "dislike Negroes because they are Negroes, but because they dislike the police department." Parker lumped all his critics with criminals, Communists, and civil rights leaders, all of whom undermined respect for the law. He had no faith in the "so-called leaders of the Negro community," he said; they used him as "their bugaboo . . .

Chief Parker

their bogeyman," their excuse for their own failure to accomplish anything. Asked how the riots began, Parker characteristically put his foot in his mouth: "One person threw a rock ... then, like monkeys in a zoo, others started throwing rocks." He disclosed his "we-they" view of the world when he remarked as the riots subsided, "Now we're on the top and they're on the bottom."[14]

Many officers on the force knew and shared Parker's outlook, including his view that the Muslims ought to be exposed as "a threat to the community." So the police were ready to believe the anonymous caller who telephoned early on the morning of Wednesday, August 18, to report that a shipment of guns had arrived at the Muslim mosque. Within minutes the building was surrounded. Somebody saw a shot flash from an upstairs window. The ring of police and guardsmen retaliated, disrupting the electrical service and shattering every window in the building. They then stormed the darkened mosque and collared twenty suspects, none of whom had

183

been injured in the furious barrage. A few moments later flames broke out, which firemen quickly knocked down.

What the firemen preserved, the police tore apart in their search for the weapons that had precipitated the raid. Pool tables, vending machines, stairwells, and partitions were dismantled without result. On the chance that a speedy Muslim had rushed the arms to the sewer, a national guard officer threw gas grenades down a manhole. Nothing flushed out any weapons, and a second fire, which investigators concluded someone had set, completed the destruction of the building's interior. Muslims believed that police had staged the entire incident, from first telephone call to final fire.

In fact, some of the violence in Watts was staged, although not very much and not the destruction of the Muslim mosque—unless

there was undisclosed evidence. A few young people threw a few bottles under the misguided direction of television cameramen, and some accomplished actors improvised rationalizations to explain their illegal activity to reporters and postriot investigators. But smoke and smashed windows and gunfire and much of the rage were real, not staged. It was as if Watts was the out-of-town tryout for the major production of violence-as-theater later in the decade, starring Black Panthers and various factions of alienated, and usually white, young people.

If there was a lesson to be learned from the ruined mosque, it was that the state could unleash more violence than could dissidents. Governor Brown's investigators estimated that about 10,000 blacks rioted, a guess other observers believed too low, but a number that was in any case no match for the retaliatory violence of 14,000 national guardsmen, nearly 1000 police, and 800 sheriff's deputies.[15] Much of the property, burned or stolen, belonged to whites, but most of the lost lives were those of blacks. The riots may have brought a little more federal money to Watts more quickly than a tranquil summer would have. But the violence that really worked was official violence, the violent defense of the status quo. Spokesmen for Mexican-Americans in Los Angeles, who had not taken to the streets in spite of living conditions that were on the average as unsatisfactory as those in Watts, warned politicians lest postriot programs for blacks seem to reward violence. They need not have worried. There were not many.

"WHO YOU WITH?"

Mayor Yorty was not receptive to federal programs anyhow. On the eve of the riots, a full year after Congress had declared war on poverty, bickering between Yorty and the Office of Economic Opportunity still blocked the allocation of antipoverty funds to Los Angeles. During the violence, the mayor charged that decisions of the Supreme Court of the United States had undermined the effort of local police to protect the city from anarchy. Yorty did not blame all blacks for the riots. Indeed, "most Negroes," he said, "deplore

185

the violence," which came from "young people roaming the streets in frustration, without jobs, without education." Robert Fogelson has labelled this explanation "the 'riffraff theory' of riot participation."[16]

This riffraff theory held that riots occurred more or less for the hell of it, out of a social malaise no more serious than individual anger. Such a Pollyanna analysis exonerated white America and required no major modification in public policy. Blacks would have to change—strengthen their marriages, curb their sexual impulses, keep their children in school, work harder, and save their money. Government, in turn, should find more money for familiar programs—public housing, public education, public assistance.[17] These devices would liberate worthy blacks, and presumably the police would dispose of the riffraff that remained.

Those who disagreed pointed out that the violence in Watts was neither random nor individual, but rather seemed almost purposeful. Many of the victims of arson and looting, for example, were

white merchants with a reputation for gouging their customers. Private dwellings, public buildings, manufacturing plants, and the businesses of black proprietors ordinarily escaped damage. Snipers, who harassed police and firemen as the riots continued, never killed anyone. Maybe there were fewer snipers than the first hysterical reports contended, or maybe they were bad marksmen. But perhaps they simply did not mean to kill anyone.

Nor does the riffraff interpretation explain either the broad participation in the riots or the support for rioters among blacks who did not themselves throw rocks and loot. Those arrested, as one study has concluded, were "in the mainstream of modern Negro urban life."[18] Dismissing them as riffraff because their mothers collected welfare, or because they were out of school and unemployed, or because they had once before been arrested, similarly stigmatized a large fraction of the urban black population.

Finally, the riffraff theory did not account for the failure of the social controls that usually prevented violence, not only in Los

Angeles in 1965 but in many other parts of the country during the rest of the decade. Order, after all, exists because leaders, self-interest, and fear inhibit those who might prefer disorder. It was conventional to blame the deterioration of those controls on the Supreme Court, inadequate parental supervision, and the child-raising theories of Dr. Benjamin Spock. Several politicians, including Vice President Spiro Agnew, made a career of campaigning against social "permissiveness," but the analysis was as shallow as those who offered it. Charging parents with laxness did not explain why they were lax, nor did it breathe new vigor into the moral consensus parents could not summon the energy to uphold. The "permissiveness" of courts derived from their attempt to strike a new balance between justice and equality on the one hand, and order on the other.

The Supreme Court and the Congress had, however, reduced the effectiveness of undisguised white racism as a tool of social control. Keeping blacks in their place became more difficult when subtler forms of discrimination had to replace restrictive housing agreements, segregated schools, and the politics of white supremacy. The gradual replacement of Uncle Tom's deference with pride that sometimes seemed truculent marked the lapse of an overt system of racial control.

If they had given up control themselves, whites nevertheless expected to select black leaders to carry on instead. President Johnson, for instance, conferred prestige on racial moderates by seeking the advice of integrationists like Martin Luther King, Jr., and Roy Wilkins of the NAACP. Through political preferment, publicity, and other rewards, whites elsewhere designated local black leaders, some of whom had less contact with rank-and-file blacks than did King and Wilkins. The riots exposed the ineffectiveness of some of this leadership and the breakdown of social controls in the ghettoes. There were random acts of unremarked heroism by those who deplored what was happening to their neighborhood: a beating stopped here, a store saved there, younger brothers or sons kept off the streets. But frequently the task was hopeless. When California Assemblyman Mervyn Dymally urged calm on a group of stone-

"Take me to a leader!"

throwing blacks, a boy stepped out of the crowd. "Who you with?" the lad asked. "I'm with you, man," answered Dymally, trying to keep some contact with his audience. "Then here's a rock, baby," came the rejoinder; "throw it."[19]

Dymally's dilemma was the dilemma of black moderates. Viewed objectively, violence seemed likely to be counterproductive. It would undermine moderate leaders whom whites respected, reduce white support for civil rights reforms, tear up the neighborhood where blacks lived and worked, and perhaps provoke the white majority to resort again to the force that had for generations suppressed the black minority. Yet there was no question that the riots caught the attention of whites in a way the demonstrations of Martin Luther King, Jr., had not. Further, the riots obviously generated a sense of pride and accomplishment among people who had too little of either. Perhaps those emotions could be guided into more acceptable channels once the riots were over.

Nationally known moderates fared no better than Dymally. Dick Gregory, a nightclub comic and civil rights activist, tried to promote

Assemblyman Mervyn M. Dymally

social justice with brave deeds and witty words. Gregory knew his ghettoes; he had been born in one in St. Louis and in 1965 lived in one in Chicago. Although Southern race relations had improved, he remarked in the summer of 1965, the Northern cities would probably "go up in smoke" before the struggle for equality ended. He was not far away when the fires began in Los Angeles, and he persuaded the police to lend him a bullhorn and take him to the trouble. For more than two hours Gregory worked the crowds, trying to convert destructive energy into concern for potential victims. The tactic did not work. A bullet hit him in the thigh. Gregory got up, approached his assailant, and asked him once more to go home. After treatment, Gregory was back at the same stand, tirelessly delivering the same message, with the same depressing lack of result.

One of the voices in one of the crowds Gregory collected shouted "We don't want Martin Luther King down here either," a jeer that brought laughing agreement. But King came anyway in a parade of new station wagons. If the vehicles were supposed to attract respectful attention, they failed. A young black took a look and remarked

191

disgustedly, "Aw, they're just sending another nigger down here to tell us what we need." King's speech was perfunctory and ineffective. His famous "I have a dream" refrain was mocked: "hell, we don't need no damn dreams," one skeptic remarked; "we want jobs." King's platitudes about better tomorrows brought an insistent "When, dammit, when?" from the crowd, and his invitation to join hands was given an unusual twist by the interruption "and burn, baby, burn." It was not the Reverend King's usual "Amen corner."[20]

King's reception in Watts demonstrated the semantic trap in the phrase "black community." In Montgomery, in 1955, there had been a black community—a group of people with common experience, shared values, and similar aspirations. But Watts in 1965 was not a community of any hue. Ministers in Montgomery had led their congregations in prayer and rallied them in the cause of civil rights; self-ordained ministers in Watts owned their churches, ran them as

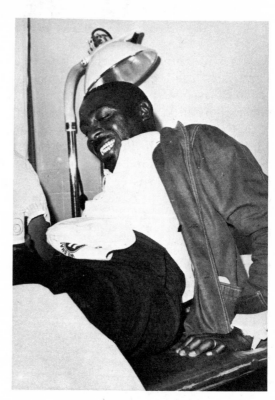

Dick Gregory awaits
treatment

Watts was not Montgomery

businesses, and pocketed the profits. Churches provided a social cohesion among blacks in Montgomery for which there was no equivalent in Watts except, perhaps, adolescent gangs. Segregation forced Montgomery's middle-class blacks to identify with other blacks in the city; middle-class blacks in Watts sought a way out.

A LOWERED VOICE

The fires were hardly cold before Governor Brown asked an investigating commission to identify the causes of the riots and to suggest policies to prevent recurrence. Because of the air of crisis, Brown asked chairman John A. McCone, a businessman with extensive governmental experience, to report promptly. In their haste, the commissioners broke no new ground and almost embraced the riffraff theory when they described the riots as "an insensate rage of destruction, . . . a spasm" that "passed."[21]

Yet while the report blamed irresponsible individuals, it also went beyond that. The commissioners worried about the gap between what the nation's underprivileged received from society and what had been promised, and then urged more and better governmental services: schools, buses, jobs, protection for consumers, and sensitive, tolerant policemen. In a sense, as the McCone Commission viewed it, the riot almost seemed an affirmation of the American system. Those who rioted, the commission believed, did not mean to reject either existing institutions or public programs, but rather to demand more from both.

The McCone Commission, like other investigations of subsequent violence in the decade, was caught between disapproval of discrimination on the one hand, and an equally strong condemnation of disorder on the other. Commissioners had to reconcile their respect for legal process with their sympathy for the undeniable grievances of blacks.[22] Investigators found various ways to walk this tightrope, an exercise that usually required the assertion that racial oppression caused frustration and violence. That proposition became part of the conventional wisdom of the decade: poverty, discrimination, segregation, inadequate public services, repressive police—life, in short, in the ghetto—produced riots.

Critics called the conclusion too conventional. A spokesman for the United Auto Workers dismissed the McCone report as "a mouse-size solution to lion-size problems." A disappointed Los Angeles black thought the $250,000 spent during McCone's inquiry would have done more good if scattered along the streets in Watts. Those who had followed the daily coverage of the riots thought the report obscured the rage and racial hostility that seemed so much a part of events as they happened. And several social scientists wondered how the commissioners could have failed to interpret violence as a revolutionary political statement—a rejection of the liberal political orthodoxy the commissioners themselves represented.[23]

Two years later, the National Advisory Commission on Civil

Disorders (called the Kerner Commission after chairman Otto Kerner, then governor of Illinois), underlined many of the McCone Commission's recommendations. The press picked the phrase "white racism" from the introduction as the Kerner Commission's chief explanation for urban riots, a simplification that was not really misleading. Although "white racism" seemed an accurate summary of what the commissioners thought, the report itself did not demonstrate the charge, a point critics quickly made. The text, they noted, provided for the umpteenth time facts about black deprivation everyone already knew, when research ought to have documented the prejudices of whites. The commission's own explanation, these readers said, required an investigation of the bigotry of white employers, rather than familiar statistics about black unemployment, and new data on the attitudes of white teachers instead of more tables recording the failures of black pupils.

Furthermore, the reforms the commission proposed seemed unrelated to the white racism that presumably caused the disturbances. When decades of liberal programs had not eliminated white racism, why would more of the same suddenly succeed? If white racism was embedded in American institutions—in the system that permitted a private employer to choose his employees, for example—what could yet another federal program accomplish? Would a miraculous cleansing of white hearts and minds convert the ghettoes to suburbs? White racism, in other words, furnished an inadequate basis for public policy because American politics is the art of the possible: in demanding the impossible—no democratic government could eliminate personal prejudice—the analysis, in effect, demanded nothing.[24]

Although several critics of the reports doubted the effectiveness of more legislation and more money, blacks seemed to welcome both. Bayard Rustin, for instance, a civil rights leader who had joined Martin Luther King, Jr., for dismaying conversations with Mayor Yorty and Chief Parker, criticized the McCone report because its endorsement of major new federal programs was too tepid. In so far as the mood of the ghettoes can be gauged, blacks wanted more of

Other cities burn:
Washington (right)
and Newark (below)

what American institutions were awarding to whites, not some new system with other rewards. That was, at least, a plausible interpretation of the way blacks talked and acted, before, during, and after the riots.

What they did was stop rioting. Not immediately, for urban violence boiled out of black neighborhoods across the country for the next two or three years. Disorder plagued Milwaukee and Omaha; Newark and Plainfield, New Jersey; Cambridge, Maryland, and Cambridge, Massachusetts; Chicago; Detroit; New York; and Washington. The disturbances usually matured from familiar grievances—segregated schools, inadequate housing, "police brutality"—and sometimes, most notably after the murder of Martin Luther King, Jr., in 1968, from spontaneous rage. Rioting did not improve housing or schools or employment opportunities and often made conditions worse. Yet the level of violence diminished after 1968.

No commission wrote a report about that, though the restoration of urban peace, in the absence of improvement, discredited the explanation of violence as a logical response to wretched conditions. Perhaps ghetto residents learned the ineffectiveness of violence from the nation's massive, and ultimately futile, use of force in Vietnam. Perhaps the novelty wore off, or the realization spread that destruction of one's own neighborhood was not a happy way to send a message to those in power. Most blacks apparently decided that riots accomplished less than political action. The civil rights movement had trained black political leaders and tested organizational techniques. After the Voting Rights Act of 1965, that experience could flow in traditional political channels.

It did not happen right away; several years passed before the public began to appreciate the impact blacks might have on the nation's politics. There were straws in the wind: more token appointments, a black caucus in the Congress, enhanced representation and influence in the Democratic party, growing numbers of black officeholders—even in the South. In the 1970s, some of the cities scarred by violence in the previous decade, including Newark, Detroit, and Los Angeles, elected black mayors. Mervyn Dymally, who had tried to disperse streetcorner dissidents during the Watts

Urban mayors of the 1970s: Mayor Thomas Bradley, Los Angeles (left) and Mayor Kenneth Gibson, Newark (right)

riots, moved up in California politics, to lieutenant governor in 1974. "You don't get anything by demanding the whole world at the top of your lungs," Andrew Young, one of the most successful of those black politicians, once remarked. Young knew, and other American blacks had learned, that a lowered voice need not imply lowered aspirations.[25]

The political success of an Andrew Young or a Mervyn Dymally did not herald an interracial utopia, any more than had integrated buses in Montgomery two decades before. Indeed, more than thirty years after the wartime riots, in spite of several blue-ribbon committees, the election of a black mayor, and the expenditure of some imagination, considerable energy, and tens of millions of dollars in Detroit, an explosive racial tension remained. Yet that discouraging fact ought not entirely to obscure another: the reforms enacted in response to the civil rights movement had changed for the better the lives of most American blacks. Reformers, out of naive idealism and their anxiety to persuade, had promised more than any legislature or

198

any legislation could deliver. Racial toleration depends at least as much upon the character of a people as upon the content of their statute books.

Yet change in the content of the statute books was worth achieving, even if prejudice remained. An interview with an employer who obeyed the law was better than no consideration at all. Admission to a hotel that had once discriminated was an advance, although others continued their illegal practices. More extensive participation by blacks in American politics constituted progress, even if some remained excluded and the political process itself remained corrupt. Something, on the whole, was better than nothing, as earlier American reformers had discovered.

Notes

[1]Jerry Cohen and William S. Murphy, *Burn, Baby, Burn!* (New York: Dutton, 1966) is based on their reporting of the riots for the *Los Angeles Times*. Robert Conot, *Rivers of Blood, Years of Darkness* (New York: Bantam, 1967) is another journalistic account.

[2]James Baldwin, *The Fire Next Time* (New York: Dial Press, 1963), p. 102.

[3]Quoted in Conot, *Rivers*, p. 186.

[4]The McCone Commission's report is contained in Robert M. Fogelson, comp., *The Los Angeles Riots* (New York: Arno Press, 1969); this quotation is from pp. 5–6.

[5]*Ibid.*, p. 77; Cohen and Murphy, *Burn*, pp. 134–36; U.S. National Commission on Civil Disorders ("Kerner Commission"), *Report . . .* (Washington, D.C.: Government Printing Office, 1968), p. 116; Conot, *Rivers*, pp. 380–81.

[6]Paul Jacobs, *Prelude to Riot* (New York: Random House, 1967), p. 6.

[7]Martin Luther King, Jr., "Next Stop: the North," in *Saturday Review*, November 13, 1965, p. 33.

[8]*McCone Report*, p. 17.

[9]Conot, *Rivers*, p. 325.

[10]*Ibid.*, pp. 229–30; Cohen and Murphy, *Burn*, pp. 211–13.

[11]Conot, *Rivers*, pp. 357–58; Cohen and Murphy, *Burn*, pp. 232–37.

[12]Conot, *Rivers*, chapters 52, 53.

[13]*Ibid.*, p. 151; cf. Cohen and Murphy, *Burn*, p. 87.

[14]Conot, *Rivers*, pp. 98–103, 348–49; Cohen and Murphy, *Burn*, pp. 296–300; *Newsweek*, August 30, 1965, p. 17; *U.S. News and World Report*, August 30, 1965, pp. 22–23.

[15]*McCone Report*, p. 20.

[16]Robert M. Fogelson, *Violence as Protest* (Garden City, N.Y.: Doubleday, 1971), p. 28; see also *McCone Report*, p. 118, and Cohen and Murphy, *Burn*, p. 130.

[17]See, for example, the recommendations of the McCone Commission in *Report*, pp. 57–88.

[18]This study, by social scientists from the University of California, Los Angeles, is quoted in Fogelson, *Violence*, p. 122.

[19]Cohen and Murphy, *Burn*, p. 119; *Time*, August 27, 1965, p. 10.

[20]Cohen and Murphy, *Burn*, pp. 119–20, 278; Conot, *Rivers*, p. 369; *Newsweek*, August 30, 1965, pp. 15, 19; King, "Next Stop," pp. 33–34.

[21]*McCone Report*, p. 1.

[22]Analysis of Allan Silver, cited in Fogelson, *Violence*, p. 160.

[23]See, for example, Robert Blauner, "Whitewash over Watts," reprinted in David Boesel and Peter H. Rossi, eds., *Cities Under Siege* (New York: Basic Books, 1971), p. 210ff.; and Bayard Rustin, "The Watts 'Manifesto' & The McCone Report," reprinted in *McCone Report*, p. 147ff. See also *Time*, December 17, 1965, p. 21.

[24]See, for example, Andrew Kopkind, "White on Black," in Boesel and Rossi, *Cities*, p. 226ff.

[25]Quoted in *New York Times*, July 14, 1976; see also *ibid.*, February 21, 1977.

EPILOGUE
Of Parables and the Present: The 1970s

So much has happened since 1965 that the riots in Watts seem a long time ago. Surprise has rapidly followed surprise, and patterns of change blur as the urgent headlines of one day merge into those of the next. Some events of the recent past hint that the nation's birthright may not include perpetual prosperity, that the moral consensus that sustains society may not endure, that our high ideals have not banished violence and intolerance and greed from the land. We have some recollection of Vietnam and Watergate; we remember imprecisely statistics about draft evasion, inflation, and drug addiction; we can still hear rhetoric about the busing of school children. We have also compressed these memories and pushed them further into the past than chronology warrants.

But we have not thereby gained historical perspective, for too much of what has happened still seems unrelated to other threads of twentieth-century American history. Taken together, for instance, the chapters of this book indicate a relatively responsive political system, gradual progress toward economic and racial justice, and a developing tolerance that permits community without requiring conformity. Of course injustice, intolerance, and corruption remain, but some of those recent events seem more than manifestations of continuing social imperfection. They challenge our easy faith in progress; they weaken our confidence in American institutions; they create uncertainty about our basic moral assumptions.

That sort of doubt dulls the urge to improve. Since reform is a major theme of American history in this century, a real loss of the reforming impulse would be significant. Reformers, after all, must believe that conscience will inspire fundamentally decent people to carry out enlightened change. That is the faith that encouraged progressives and prohibitionists to find legislative solutions to the evils of factories and saloons. That is the faith that sustained New Dealers and the postwar "New Negroes." And that is the faith that violence in Watts, and several events since, has shaken.

Yet the violence of Watts, and much of the violence related in this book, did not bespeak the desire of the underprivileged for another socioeconomic system so much as envy of what the existing system awarded to others. Wobblies in Lawrence and rioters in Watts did not disparage the goal reformers sought so much as delay in achieving it. Brought up to believe that violence is somehow subversive, Americans have not always realized that link between reform and violence. By dramatizing the anarchic alternatives to prudent change, violence may even enhance the appeal of reformers, in the same way that urban violence in the late 1960s stimulated increased political participation by blacks.

As the passionate controversies about Prohibition and labor unions now seem curious and dated, so the years that remain in the twentieth century will at least take the surprise, and probably much of the sting, from contemporary events. Most of them will in retrospect become simply one more example of familiar historical trends.

But a few of those events, because they evoke the moment or because they point toward the future, will become parables for historians. Even the best-informed observer cannot now distinguish the significant from the transitory or select the example that best illustrates a decade. Our historical filter traps random facts. We collect notes toward a history of our time, not data ready for instant analysis; we offer conjectures, not conclusions.

Some of those conjectures will one day seem as foolish as Henry Ford's guess that the Wagner Act would be held unconstitutional or Jack Crenshaw's bet that Montgomery's blacks would falter. Perhaps, for instance, new technology will make contemporary concern about a shortage of energy seem as unnecessary as worry about the radicalism of immigrants early in the century. Perhaps, on the other hand, a local crisis over construction of a nuclear power plant will one day effectively illustrate the nation's attempt to balance demands for energy and economic growth with the conflicting desire not to damage irreparably the surrounding countryside. Similarly, the economic setbacks of the 1970s may eventually appear to have been a temporary dip, much less significant than the depression of the 1930s. Or it may be that the expansion of an air base, or the failure of an electronics firm to compete with imported products, or a demonstration demanding equal pay for female employees will eventually seem evidence of economic developments as fundamental as the stock market's collapse in 1929. Possibly the decay of Northern cities did not herald a permanent shift of the nation's center of economic gravity toward the South and Southwest. Yet many of the problems of Phoenix and Atlanta and Houston stemmed from growth that Trenton and Buffalo and Hartford would have welcomed.

New York City, for a century and a half the symbol of American vitality, had more perils than Pauline. If the city escaped bankruptcy and bureaucracy and lawlessness and pollution, its survival would have symbolic significance as well. None of New York's crises were typical because no other community lived on New York's scale. But if New York could meet them, then any community might reasonably hope to find a sensible way around the obstacles it faced.

That was the sort of hope that had nurtured American reform in the twentieth century. Those who had expected radical change from a strike in Lawrence or a demonstration in Detroit or a riot in Watts lived in fantasy. But better wages and increased municipal assistance for the unemployed and enhanced recognition of racial injustice constituted progress, if not paradise. The United States was not the best of all possible worlds, but gradually it became better than it had been.

Viewed incident by incident, decade by decade, that improvement is sometimes obscured. Yet when the incidents and the decades run together and permit a comparison of the present with life when the century opened, the country's substantial effort to live up to its ideals shows clearly. That should hearten those who want to keep trying.

PHOTO CREDITS

205

Index

Figures in italics refer to illustrations.

211

A 7
B 8
C 9
D 0
E 1
F 2
G 3
H 4
I 5
J 6